NO FEAR SHAKESPEARE

NO FEAR SHAKESPEARE

NO FEAR SHAKESPEARE

THE TAMING OF THE SHREW

SPARK NOTES

The original text and translation for this edition was prepared by John Crowther.

Spark Publishing
A Division of Barnes & Noble
120 Fifth Avenue
New York, NY 10011
www.sparknotes.com

Please submit changes or report errors to www.sparknotes.com/errors

Library of Congress Cataloging-in-Publication

Shakespeare, William, 1564–1616.
  The taming of the shrew.
    p. cm. — (No fear Shakespeare)
  ISBN-13: 978-1-4114-0100-6

1. Man-woman relationships—Juvenile drama. 2. Married people—Juvenile drama.
3. Padua (Italy)—Juvenile drama. 4. Sex role—Juvenile drama. 5. Children's plays, English.
[1. Plays.] I. Title. PR2832.A25 2004
822.3'3—dc22

                                    2004000331

Printed and bound in the United States

15 14 13 S N 35 34 33 32 31

There's matter in these sighs, these profound heaves.
You must translate: 'tis fit we understand them.

(Hamlet, 4.1.1–2)

FEAR NOT.

Have you ever found yourself looking at a Shakespeare play, then down at the footnotes, then back at the play, and still not understanding? You know what the individual words mean, but they don't add up. SparkNotes' *No Fear Shakespeare* will help you break through all that. Put the pieces together with our easy-to-read translations. Soon you'll be reading Shakespeare's own words fearlessly—and actually enjoying it.

No Fear Shakespeare puts Shakespeare's language side-by-side with a facing-page translation into modern English— the kind of English people actually speak today. When Shakespeare's words make your head spin, our translation will help you sort out what's happening, who's saying what, and why.

THE TAMING OF THE SHREW

CHARACTERS

Induction

Christopher Sly—A poor vagrant who falls asleep drunk in front of a tavern at the beginning of the Induction. A Lord returning from hunting finds Sly asleep and plays a trick on him, carrying Sly to the Lord's house and ordering the servants to treat Sly like a lord when he wakes up. A group of actors who visit the Lord's house perform *The Taming of the Shrew* for Sly, which takes up the rest of the play. Sly is cantankerous and quarrelsome, more interested in drinking the beer and eating the beef jerky he is used to than in accepting the role of aristocrat. However, when he finds out that in his role as a lord he has a wife (actually the Page in disguise), he quickly changes his mind, anxious to get alone with her and take her to bed.

Lord—A very wealthy nobleman whose practical joke on Sly dominates the Induction and provides the set-up for the rest of the play. As the Lord carries out his joke, making Sly think that Sly is really a lord and doesn't remember it, we get to see all of the luxuries that an aristocrat of Shakespeare's day would enjoy—a pack of hunting dogs, numerous servants, a grand house, erotic artwork, imported wines and perfumes, preserved fruits, and so on.

Hostess—The proprietress of a tavern who gets in an argument with Sly in the first lines of the play.

Page—A boy servant to the Lord. The Lord has the Page dress as a lady and play the part of Sly's wife.

Players—A troupe of traveling actors who arrive at the Lord's house offering to perform, and who help the Lord carry out his joke on Sly. They perform *The Taming of the Shrew*.

The Play

Katherine—The shrew of the play's title, and the oldest daughter of Baptista Minola and sister of Bianca. Katherine, who is also called Katherina or Kate, is extremely strong-willed. She insists upon saying whatever she thinks and expressing whatever she feels. Her words are abusive and angry, and her actions are often violent. In Shakespeare's time, women like Katherine were called shrews, and they were strongly disapproved of as the worst possible kind of women. Petruchio undertakes the challenge of taming her, turning her into an obedient and pleasant wife.

Petruchio—A wealthy gentleman from Verona. Loud, boisterous, eccentric, and quick-witted, Petruchio comes to Padua to increase his fortune by marrying rich. All he wants is a bride with an enormous dowry, and Katherine fits the bill. Though everyone else warns him against trying to marry Katherine, he sets out to tame her by pitting his own violent temper against hers.

Baptista Minola—A wealthy citizen of Padua, and the father of Katherine and Bianca. Though many men want to marry Bianca, Baptista refuses to allow Bianca to marry before Katherine, whom no one wants to marry. Baptista is good-hearted and generous toward his two daughters, lavishing expensive books and lessons upon them, but he is completely at a loss for how to deal with the strong-willed Katherine.

Bianca—The younger daughter of Baptista. The opposite of her sister Katherine, Bianca is soft-spoken, sweet, and unassuming, as well as beautiful. Because of her large dowry and her mild behavior, several men compete for her hand.

Lucentio—A young nobleman from Pisa who comes to Padua to study at the city's renowned university, but who is immediately sidetracked when he falls in love with Bianca at first sight. Good-natured and intrepid, Lucentio is the most sympathetic of Bianca's suitors. He disguises himself as a classics instructor named Cambio so he can gain access to Bianca and win her love.

Tranio—Lucentio's servant, who accompanies Lucentio from Pisa. Wily and comical, Tranio plays an important part in Lucentio's charade by pretending to be Lucentio and bargaining with Baptista for Bianca's hand.

Gremio and **Hortensio**—Two older gentlemen of Padua who want to marry Bianca. Although they are rivals, they become allies because of their mutual frustration with and rejection by Bianca. Hortensio is an old friend of Petruchio's, and he suggests Katherine as a possible wife for Petruchio. He then dresses up as a music instructor to court Bianca. Hortensio and Gremio are both thwarted by Lucentio in their efforts to win Bianca.

Grumio—Petruchio's servant and the fool of the play. He provides comic relief by pretending to misunderstand Petruchio and getting into ridiculous arguments with him.

Biondello—Lucentio's second servant, who assists his master and Tranio in carrying out their plot.

Curtis, **Nathaniel**, **Phillip**, **Joseph**, **Nicholas**, **Peter**— Servants in Petruchio's household.

Tailor, **Haberdasher**—The dress-maker and hat-maker hired by Petruchio to dress Katherine. Petruchio criticizes their work and sends them away, as part of his scheme to tame Katherine.

Widow—A wealthy widow of Padua whom Hortensio marries after abandoning his attempt to marry Bianca.

Merchant—A merchant recently from Mantua, whom Lucentio tricks into pretending to be Lucentio's father.

INDUCTION
SCENE 1

Enter SLY *and* HOSTESS

SLY

I'll pheeze you, in faith.

HOSTESS

A pair of stocks, you rogue!

SLY

Y'are a baggage, the Slys are no rogues. Look in
the chronicles—we came in with Richard Conqueror.
5   Therefore *paucas pallabris*: let the world slide. Sessa!

HOSTESS

You will not pay for the glasses you have burst?

SLY

No, not a denier. Go by, Saint Jeronimy. Go to thy cold bed
and warm thee.

HOSTESS

I know my remedy. I must go fetch the thirdborough.

Exit

SLY

10   Third, or fourth, or fifth borough, I'll answer him by law.
I'll not budge an inch, boy. Let him come, and kindly.

Falls asleep

Wind horns

Enter a LORD *from hunting, with his train*

INDUCTION
SCENE 1

SLY *and* HOSTESS *enter.*

SLY

I'll fix you, I swear.

HOSTESS

You thug! I'll call for a pair of stocks!

SLY

There are no thugs in my family, whore! Read your history! We Slys came over with Richard the Conqueror. Oh, the hell with it. I can't be bothered. Shut up!

HOSTESS

You won't pay for the glasses you smashed?

SLY

No, not a penny. Get out of my face. Go play with yourself.

HOSTESS

I know my rights. I'll call a policeman.

She exits.

SLY

Call them all! I have a legal right to be here. I'm not moving an inch, pal. Let them come—I don't care.

He falls asleep.

A hunting horn is heard. A LORD *who has been hunting enters with his hunstmen.*

LORD

Huntsman, I charge thee, tender well my hounds.
Breathe Merriman, the poor cur is embossed,
And couple Clowder with the deep-mouthed brach.
15   Saw'st thou not, boy, how Silver made it good
At the hedge corner, in the coldest fault?
I would not lose the dog for twenty pound.

FIRST HUNTSMAN

Why, Belman is as good as he, my lord.
He cried upon it at the merest loss,
20   And twice today picked out the dullest scent.
Trust me, I take him for the better dog.

LORD

Thou art a fool. If Echo were as fleet,
I would esteem him worth a dozen such.
But sup them well and look unto them all.
25   Tomorrow I intend to hunt again.

FIRST HUNTSMAN

I will, my lord.

LORD

What's here? One dead, or drunk? See, doth he breathe?

SECOND HUNTSMAN

He breathes, my lord. Were he not warmed with ale,
This were a bed but cold to sleep so soundly.

LORD

30   O monstrous beast, how like a swine he lies!
Grim death, how foul and loathsome is thine image!
Sirs, I will practice on this drunken man.
What think you: if he were conveyed to bed,
Wrapped in sweet clothes, rings put upon his fingers,
35   A most delicious banquet by his bed,
And brave attendants near him when he wakes,
Would not the beggar then forget himself?

LORD

Huntsman, look after my hounds. Let Merriman catch his breath—the poor dog's foaming at the mouth. And tie up Clowder together with the long-mouthed bitch. *(to his page)* Did you see, boy, how Silver picked up the scent at the hedge corner, where it was weakest? I wouldn't part with that dog for twenty pounds.

FIRST HUNTSMAN

I think Belman is just as good, my lord. He set up a howl when the scent was lost completely and twice picked it up where it was weakest. I swear he's the better dog.

LORD

You're a fool. If Echo were as fast, he would be worth a dozen like Belman. But give them all a good dinner and look after them well. I'll go hunting again tomorrow, I think.

FIRST HUNTSMAN

I will, my lord.

LORD

What's this? A drunkard or a corpse? Check and see if he's breathing.

SECOND HUNTSMAN

He is, my lord. But this would be too cold a place to sleep if he hadn't warmed himself with ale.

LORD

It's disgusting, sleeping that way—like a pig in the gutter! Alas, grim death, how vile and ugly your near-twin, sleep, is! Gentlemen, I think I'll play a trick on this lout. What do you think? Say we were to carry him to one of the bedrooms, put fresh clothes on him and rings on his fingers, lay out a wonderful feast by his bed, and have servants in fancy dress near him when he wakes up—wouldn't the poor tramp be confused?

FIRST HUNTSMAN
Believe me, lord, I think he cannot choose.

SECOND HUNTSMAN
It would seem strange unto him when he waked.

LORD
40 Even as a flatt'ring dream or worthless fancy.
Then take him up and manage well the jest.
Carry him gently to my fairest chamber
And hang it round with all my wanton pictures.
Balm his foul head in warm distilled waters
45 And burn sweet wood to make the lodging sweet.
Procure me music ready when he wakes,
To make a dulcet and a heavenly sound.
And if he chance to speak, be ready straight
And with a low submissive reverence
50 Say, "What is it your Honor will command?"
Let one attend him with a silver basin
Full of rose-water and bestrewed with flowers,
Another bear the ewer, the third a diaper,
And say, "Will 't please your Lordship cool your hands?"
55 Someone be ready with a costly suit
And ask him what apparel he will wear.
Another tell him of his hounds and horse,
And that his lady mourns at his disease.
Persuade him that he hath been lunatic,
60 And when he says he is, say that he dreams,
For he is nothing but a mighty lord.
This do, and do it kindly, gentle sirs.
It will be pastime passing excellent
If it be husbanded with modesty.

FIRST HUNTSMAN
65 My lord, I warrant you we will play our part
As he shall think by our true diligence
He is no less than what we say he is.

FIRST HUNTSMAN
> I don't think he'd have any choice, my lord.

SECOND HUNTSMAN
> When he woke, he wouldn't know where he was.

LORD
> It would be just like a nice daydream or fantasy. Well, take him on up and we'll try to pull it off. Carry him to my best room—gently, so he doesn't wake—and hang all my erotic paintings around him. Bathe his filthy head with warm, scented water. Burn fragrant wood to give the room a pleasant smell, and have musicians at hand, ready to produce sweet, soothing sounds when he awakes. You want to be ready in case he speaks. If he does, bow low and say deferentially, "What would your Honor have us do?" Have one servant wait on him with a basin of rosewater (throw in some petals), have another servant carry a pitcher, and a third a cloth. Say, "Would your Lordship care to freshen up?" Have someone standing by with expensive clothes, and ask him what he'd care to wear. Have another servant tell him about the dogs and horses that he owns and that his wife is grief-stricken over his illness. Convince him that he has been out of his mind—and when he says he's out of his mind *now*, tell him he's mistaken and that he is in fact a mighty lord. Do this—make it convincing—and we'll have fun. It could work if it's done subtly.

FIRST HUNTSMAN
> My lord, I promise we will play our parts so skillfully that he will believe everything we tell him.

LORD
>Take him up gently, and to bed with him,
>And each one to his office when he wakes.

>*Some servants carry out* SLY. *Sound trumpets*

70   Sirrah, go see what trumpet 'tis that sounds.

>*Exit Servingman*

>Belike some noble gentleman that means,
>Traveling some journey, to repose him here.

>*Enter* SERVANT

>How now! who is it?

SERVANT
>   An 't please your Honor, players
>That offer service to your Lordship.

LORD
75   Bid them come near.

>*Enter* PLAYERS

>Now, fellows, you are welcome.

PLAYERS
>We thank your Honor.

LORD
>Do you intend to stay with me tonight?

A PLAYER
>So please your Lordship to accept our duty.

LORD
80   With all my heart. This fellow I remember
>Since once he played a farmer's eldest son.
>'Twas where you wooed the gentlewoman so well.
>I have forgot your name, but sure that part
>Was aptly fitted and naturally performed.

LORD

Carry him gently to bed, and every man be ready at his post when he awakes.

Several servants carry SLY *out. Trumpets sound.*

Go, lad, and find out what the trumpet's sounding for.

A servant exits.

It's probably some noble gentleman stopping off in mid-journey, thinking to spend the night here.

A SERVANT *enters.*

Well, who is it?

SERVANT

Sir, it's a troupe of actors who want to perform for your Lordship.

LORD

Have them come in.

The PLAYERS *(actors) enter.*

You are welcome here, my friends.

PLAYERS

We thank your Honor.

LORD

Were you thinking of spending the night here?

A PLAYER

Yes, if that would be all right with your Lordship.

LORD

By all means. I remember this fellow—he once played the eldest son of a farmer. It was the play in which you wooed the gentlewoman so successfully. I have forgotten your name, but you were well cast in the role and played it convincingly.

A PLAYER

85   I think 'twas Soto that your Honor means.

LORD

'Tis very true. Thou didst it excellent.
Well, you are come to me in happy time,
The rather for I have some sport in hand
Wherein your cunning can assist me much.
90   There is a lord will hear you play tonight;
But I am doubtful of your modesties,
Lest over-eyeing of his odd behavior—
For yet his Honor never heard a play—
You break into some merry passion
95   And so offend him. For I tell you, sirs,
If you should smile, he grows impatient.

A PLAYER

Fear not, my lord, we can contain ourselves
Were he the veriest antic in the world.

LORD

Go, sirrah, take them to the buttery
100   And give them friendly welcome every one.
Let them want nothing that my house affords.

Exit one with the **PLAYERS**

Sirrah, go you to Barthol'mew, my page,
And see him dressed in all suits like a lady.
That done, conduct him to the drunkard's chamber
105   And call him "madam," do him obeisance.
Tell him from me, as he will win my love,
He bear himself with honorable action,
Such as he hath observed in noble ladies
Unto their lords, by them accomplishèd.

A PLAYER

I believe your Honor is thinking of a character called Soto.

LORD

Yes, that was it. You gave an excellent performance. Well, this is very fortunate, your arriving just at this moment. I happen to be planning a little entertainment and could really use your services. There is a particular lord who will watch you perform tonight. I'm a little worried, though—because his Honor has never seen a play before—that his odd behavior may strike you as funny. You might not be able to control your laughter and you might offend him. I warn you, he's sensitive. The slightest smile provokes him.

A PLAYER

Don't worry. We'll restrain ourselves—no matter how bizarrely he behaves.

LORD

Go, lad, and take them to the pantry. Make them feel welcome and see to it that they have everything they require.

A servant exits with the PLAYERS.

You, fellow, go fetch my page, Bartholomew, and dress him up like a noble lady. When you've finished, bring him to the drunkard's room, address him as "madam," bow to him and treat him with all-round respect and deference, as though he were the lady of the house. Give him this message: if he wants to please me, he will conduct himself like a member of the aristocracy, mimicking the kind of behavior he's seen noble ladies use toward their husbands.

110   Such duty to the drunkard let him do
       With soft low tongue and lowly courtesy,
       And say, "What is 't your Honor will command,
       Wherein your lady and your humble wife
       May show her duty and make known her love?"
115   And then with kind embracements, tempting kisses,
       And with declining head into his bosom,
       Bid him shed tears, as being overjoyed
       To see her noble lord restored to health,
       Who for this seven years hath esteemed him
120   No better than a poor and loathsome beggar.
       And if the boy have not a woman's gift
       To rain a shower of commanded tears,
       An onion will do well for such a shift,
       Which in a napkin being close conveyed
125   Shall in despite enforce a watery eye.
       See this dispatched with all the haste thou canst:
       Anon I'll give thee more instructions.

Exit a servingman

       I know the boy will well usurp the grace,
       Voice, gait, and action of a gentlewoman.
130   I long to hear him call the drunkard "husband,"
       And how my men will stay themselves from laughter
       When they do homage to this simple peasant.
       I'll in to counsel them. Haply my presence
       May well abate the over-merry spleen
135   Which otherwise would grow into extremes.

Exeunt

That's just how I want him to behave toward the drunkard, speaking in a low, soft voice and in humble, courteous tones and saying fancy stuff like, "What does your Honor wish to command your lady, your humble wife, to do to show her devotion and demonstrate her love?" Tell him to give the drunkard fond embraces and alluring kisses, and lay his head on the other man's breast, weeping like a woman overjoyed to see a husband restored to health who for the last seven years has imagined he was no better than a poor, pathetic beggar. The boy may lack a woman's gift for weeping at will, so it might be good to have an onion handy, hidden in a handkerchief. That'll make his eyes stream. Get this done as quickly as you can. I'll give you more instructions later.

A servant exits.

I know the boy will be a convincing gentlewoman, taking up her exact walk and talk and gentle gestures. I can't wait to hear him call the drunkard "husband," and to watch my men smother their laughter as they pay their respects to this simple peasant. I'll go and coach them. My presence may put a damper on their high spirits, which might otherwise get out of control.

They all exit.

INDUCTION, SCENE 2

Enter aloft SLY, *the drunkard, with Attendants, some with apparel, others with basin and ewer and other appurtenances, and* LORD *dressed as an attendant*

SLY
For God's sake, a pot of small ale.

FIRST SERVANT
Will 't please your Lordship drink a cup of sack?

SECOND SERVANT
Will 't please your Honor taste of these conserves?

THIRD SERVANT
What raiment will your Honor wear today?

SLY
5   I am Christophero Sly. Call not me "Honor" nor "Lordship." I ne'er drank sack in my life. An if you give me any conserves, give me conserves of beef. Ne'er ask me what raiment I'll wear, for I have no more doublets than backs, no more stockings than legs, nor no more shoes than
10   feet, nay sometime more feet than shoes, or such shoes as my toes look through the over-leather.

LORD
Heaven cease this idle humor in your Honor!
Oh, that a mighty man of such descent,
Of such possessions and so high esteem,
15   Should be infusèd with so foul a spirit!

INDUCTION, SCENE 2

SLY *appears above the stage. He is attended by several servants, some carrying clothing and others a basin, pitcher, and other accessories. The* LORD *also enters disguised as a servant.*

SLY

For God's sake, would someone bring me a mug of beer!

FIRST SERVANT

Wouldn't your Lordship prefer some imported wine?

SECOND SERVANT

Would your Honor like to try this dried fruit?

THIRD SERVANT

What garment would your Honor like to wear today?

SLY

I'm Christopher Sly. Don't call me "your Honor" and "your Lordship." I've never had imported wine in my life, and if you want to bring me something "dried," try beef jerky. Why ask me what "garment" I'll wear? I have no more jackets than I have backs, no more leggings than I have legs, and no more shoes than I have feet—in fact, sometimes I have *fewer* shoes than feet, as I'm not sure the ones where my toes stick out can be called "shoes."

LORD

May Heaven put an end to this foolish fantasy of your Honor's! How terrible that a man of your influence and noble family, with so much wealth and an excellent reputation, should be infected with such a horrible illness!

SLY
What, would you make me mad? Am not I Christopher Sly,
old Sly's son of Burton Heath, by birth a peddler, by
education a cardmaker, by transmutation a bearherd, and
now by present profession a tinker? Ask Marian Hacket,
20   the fat alewife of Wincot, if she know me not! If she say I
am not fourteen pence on the score for sheer ale, score me
up for the lying'st knave in Christendom. What! I am not
bestraught! Here's—

THIRD SERVANT
Oh, this it is that makes your lady mourn!

SECOND SERVANT
25   Oh, this is it that makes your servants droop!

LORD
Hence comes it that your kindred shuns your house,
As beaten hence by your strange lunacy.
O noble lord, bethink thee of thy birth,
Call home thy ancient thoughts from banishment,
30   And banish hence these abject lowly dreams.
Look how thy servants do attend on thee,
Each in his office ready at thy beck.
Wilt thou have music? Hark! Apollo plays,

Music

And twenty cagèd nightingales do sing:
35   Or wilt thou sleep? We'll have thee to a couch
Softer and sweeter than the lustful bed
On purpose trimmed up for Semiramis.
Say thou wilt walk, we will bestrew the ground.
Or wilt thou ride? Thy horses shall be trapped,
40   Their harness studded all with gold and pearl.
Dost thou love hawking? Thou hast hawks will soar
Above the morning lark. Or wilt thou hunt?

SLY

What, are you trying to make me crazy? I'm Christopher Sly, son of old Sly of Barton-on-Heath, a peddler by birth, a cardmaker by trade, a keeper of trained bears by bad luck, and now, by present profession, a tinker. Go ask Marian Hacket, the fat innkeeper of Wincot. She knows me! She'll tell you about the tab I've run up—fourteen pence just for ale. If she doesn't, call me the biggest liar in Christendom. I'm not crazy! Just look at how—

A cardmaker made tools for working with wool.

THIRD SERVANT

Oh, this is why your poor wife is mourning!

SECOND SERVANT

And this is why your servants hang their heads in sorrow!

LORD

And this is why your relatives never visit, frightened away by this unnatural insanity of yours. Oh noble lord, consider your lineage. Try to recall your former state of mental health and forget these crass, lowly desires. Look how your servants wait on you, each one ready to do whatever you command. Would you care to hear some music? Listen! That's Apollo playing.

Apollo was the Greek god of music and song.

Music plays.

And those birds you hear—twenty caged nightingales. Do you want to sleep? We'll have a couch made up that's softer and more fragrant even than the bed of lustful Semiramis. Say you want to take a walk, and we'll sprinkle the ground with flowers. Or do you want to go horseback riding? Your horses will be adorned with harnesses decorated in gold and pearls. Do you like hawking? You have hawks that can soar higher than the morning lark. Or do you want to hunt?

Semiramis was an Assyrian queen famous for her active sex life.

Thy hounds shall make the welkin answer them
And fetch shrill echoes from the hollow earth.

FIRST SERVANT
45   Say thou wilt course. Thy greyhounds are as swift
As breathed stags, ay, fleeter than the roe.

SECOND SERVANT
Dost thou love pictures? We will fetch thee straight
Adonis painted by a running brook
And Cytherea all in sedges hid,
50   Which seem to move and wanton with her breath,
Even as the waving sedges play with wind.

LORD
We'll show thee Io as she was a maid
And how she was beguilèd and surprised,
As lively painted as the deed was done.

THIRD SERVANT
55   Or Daphne roaming through a thorny wood,
Scratching her legs that one shall swear she bleeds,
And at that sight shall sad Apollo weep,
So workmanly the blood and tears are drawn.

LORD
Thou art a lord, and nothing but a lord.
60   Thou hast a lady far more beautiful
Than any woman in this waning age.

FIRST SERVANT
And till the tears that she hath shed for thee
Like envious floods o'errun her lovely face,
She was the fairest creature in the world—
65   And yet she is inferior to none.

Your hounds will make the sky echo with their high-pitched voices.

FIRST SERVANT

If you care to hunt rabbits, your greyhounds are as swift as healthy stags and faster than young deer.

SECOND SERVANT

Do you like pictures? We'll be right back with one of Adonis stretched out beside a rushing brook, with Venus spying on him, hidden in rushes that seem to move and undulate with her lustful sighs, like grass waving in the wind.

Adonis was a handsome mortal youth loved by Venus, the goddess of love. Cytherea is another name for Venus (in Greek, Aphrodite).

LORD

Io was a mortal girl whom the god Zeus (called Jupiter by Romans) raped. Out of jealousy, Zeus's wife transformed her into a cow.

There's one that shows Io as a maid, before she was turned into a cow, in which Jupiter tricks and takes her. It's so realistic, it seems to be happening right before your eyes.

THIRD SERVANT

Daphne was a nymph whom Apollo loved and changed into a tree as she was trying to escape from him.

There's one of Daphne running through the woods, her legs so scratched by thorns that Apollo himself would weep at the sight. You'll swear the blood and tears are real.

LORD

You are nothing less than a lord. You have a noble wife who is much more beautiful than any other woman in this declining age.

FIRST SERVANT

Before she began shedding tears all over her lovely face, she was the fairest creature in the world—and even now she has no equal.

SLY

Am I a lord, and have I such a lady?
Or do I dream? Or have I dreamed till now?
I do not sleep: I see, I hear, I speak.
I smell sweet savors and I feel soft things.
70   Upon my life, I am a lord indeed
And not a tinker, nor Christopher Sly.
Well, bring our lady hither to our sight,
And once again, a pot o' the smallest ale.

SECOND SERVANT

Will 't please your Mightiness to wash your hands?
75   O, how we joy to see your wit restored!
O, that once more you knew but what you are!
These fifteen years you have been in a dream
Or, when you waked, so waked as if you slept.

SLY

These fifteen years! By my fay, a goodly nap.
80   But did I never speak of all that time?

FIRST SERVANT

O, yes, my lord, but very idle words.
For though you lay here in this goodly chamber,
Yet would you say ye were beaten out of door;
And rail upon the hostess of the house,
85   And say you would present her at the leet,
Because she brought stone jugs and no sealed quarts.
Sometimes you would call out for Cicely Hacket.

SLY

Ay, the woman's maid of the house.

THIRD SERVANT

Why, sir, you know no house nor no such maid,
90   Nor no such men as you have reckoned up,
As Stephen Sly and old John Naps of Greece,
And Peter Turph and Henry Pimpernell,
And twenty more such names and men as these,
Which never were, nor no man ever saw.

SLY

I'm really a lord? And do I really have a wife like that? Is *this* a dream? Or has everything up till now been a dream? I don't seem to be asleep: I can see and hear and speak. I can smell sweet smells and feel things that are soft to the touch. I'll be damned! I guess I really am a lord and not a tinker, and not Christopher Sly, either. Well, bring my wife to me. Oh, and don't forget the beer.

SECOND SERVANT

Would your Mightiness care to wash his hands? We're overjoyed to see you sane again. If only you had a clearer memory of who you are! These past fifteen years you have been living in a dream, and even when you were awake, it was as though you slept.

SLY

Fifteen years! That's some nap. But I never spoke the whole time?

FIRST SERVANT

Oh yes, you spoke, my lord, but total nonsense. For instance, you'd be lying here in this comfortable room, but you'd *say* that you were being thrown out of some tavern and would shout at a landlady about how you were going to take her to court for cheating you. Sometimes you would call out for one Cicely Hacket.

SLY

Yes, the landlady's maid.

THIRD SERVANT

But sir, there is no such house, no such maid, and no such men as you have dreamed up, like a certain Stephen Sly and one old John Naps of Greece, a Peter Turph, one "Henry Pimpernell," and twenty more men of this sort—who never actually existed.

SLY

95 Now Lord be thanked for my good amends!

ALL

Amen.

SLY

I thank thee. Thou shalt not lose by it.

Enter the PAGE *as a lady, with attendants*

PAGE

How fares my noble lord?

SLY

Marry, I fare well,
For here is cheer enough. Where is my wife?

PAGE

100 Here, noble lord. What is thy will with her?

SLY

Are you my wife and will not call me "husband"?
My men should call me "lord." I am your goodman.

PAGE

My husband and my lord, my lord and husband,
I am your wife in all obedience.

SLY

105 I know it well.—What must I call her?

LORD

"Madam."

SLY

"Alice Madam," or "Joan Madam"?

LORD

"Madam," and nothing else. So lords call ladies.

SLY

Well, thank God I'm cured!

ALL

Amen.

SLY

I thank you all. You won't regret this.

The PAGE *enters, disguised as a noble lady and accompanied by servants.*

PAGE

How is my noble lord?

SLY

Not bad, actually. This is all quite pleasant. Where is my wife?

PAGE

Here, noble lord. What is your wish with regard to her?

SLY

You call yourself my wife, yet you don't call me "husband"? It's my men who should call me "lord." I'm your man, your fellow.

PAGE

My husband *is* my lord and my lord is my husband. For I am your all-obedient wife.

SLY

Yes, I see.—*(to the* LORD*)* What should I call her?

LORD

"Madam."

SLY

"Madam Alice?" Or "Madam Joan?"

Sly is asking what her name is. He doesn't understand that "Madam" is like "Sir," or "My lord."

LORD

Just "madam." That's how noblemen address their wives.

SLY
> Madam wife, they say that I have dreamed
> And slept above some fifteen year or more.

PAGE
110 Ay, and the time seems thirty unto me,
> Being all this time abandoned from your bed.

SLY
> 'Tis much.—Servants, leave me and her alone.
> Madam, undress you and come now to bed.

PAGE
> Thrice noble lord, let me entreat of you
115 To pardon me yet for a night or two,
> Or if not so, until the sun be set.
> For your physicians have expressly charged,
> In peril to incur your former malady,
> That I should yet absent me from your bed.
120 I hope this reason stands for my excuse.

SLY
> Ay, it stands so that I may hardly tarry so long. But I would
> be loath to fall into my dreams again. I will therefore tarry
> in despite of the flesh and the blood.

Enter a MESSENGER

MESSENGER
> Your Honor's players, hearing your amendment,
125 Are come to play a pleasant comedy,
> For so your doctors hold it very meet,
> Seeing too much sadness hath congealed your blood,
> And melancholy is the nurse of frenzy.
> Therefore they thought it good you hear a play
130 And frame your mind to mirth and merriment,
> Which bars a thousand harms and lengthens life.

SLY

Madam wife, they say I've been dreaming or asleep for more than fifteen years.

PAGE

Yes, and it seemed twice as long to me, having been kept from your bed that whole time.

SLY

That's too long.—Servants, leave her and me alone. Now, madam, undress and come to bed.

PAGE

Thrice noble lord, I beg you to excuse me for another night or two—or at least until nightfall. Your doctors have expressly forbidden me to sleep with you, as there's a risk that you might have a relapse. I hope this explanation will stand as my excuse.

SLY

Sly means that he is sexually aroused.

Well, something's standing up. I'm not sure I can wait that long. Still, I'd hate to see my former dreams return. So I *will* wait, however flesh and blood may feel about it.

A MESSENGER *enters.*

MESSENGER

Your Honor's actors, hearing of your recovery, have come to perform a pleasing comedy for you—and your doctors approve wholeheartedly. They say that too much suffering has made your blood coagulate, and that sadness leads to madness. So they think it's a good idea for you to watch a play and direct your thoughts toward laughter and merriment—two strong preventive medicines that foster long life.

SLY

Marry, I will. Let them play it. Is not a comonty a
Christmas gambold or a tumbling-trick?

PAGE

No, my good lord, it is more pleasing stuff.

SLY

135   What, household stuff?

PAGE

It is a kind of history.

SLY

Well, we'll see 't. Come, madam wife, sit by my side and let
the world slip. We shall ne'er be younger.

They sit

SLY

With "comonty," Sly is trying to say "comedy" but gets the word wrong, never having heard it before.

Okay, bring on the play. But what's a "comonty?" Some sort of Christmas skit or display of acrobatics?

PAGE

No, my good lord, this is nicer stuff.

SLY

What, like stuff from a house?

PAGE

No, it's a story.

SLY

Well, let's watch it. Come, madam wife, sit here beside me. Let's forget our cares. We're not getting any younger.

They sit.

ACT ONE

SCENE 1

Flourish. Enter LUCENTIO *and his man* TRANIO

LUCENTIO

Tranio, since for the great desire I had
To see fair Padua, nursery of arts,
I am arrived for fruitful Lombardy,
The pleasant garden of great Italy,
And by my father's love and leave am armed
With his goodwill and thy good company.
My trusty servant, well approved in all,
Here let us breathe and haply institute
A course of learning and ingenious studies.
Pisa, renownèd for grave citizens,
Gave me my being and my father first,
A merchant of great traffic through the world,
Vincentio, come of the Bentivolii.
Vincentio's son, brought up in Florence,
It shall become to serve all hopes conceived
To deck his fortune with his virtuous deeds.
And therefore, Tranio, for the time I study
Virtue, and that part of philosophy
Will I apply that treats of happiness
By virtue specially to be achieved.
Tell me thy mind, for I have Pisa left
And am to Padua come, as he that leaves
A shallow plash to plunge him in the deep
And with satiety seeks to quench his thirst.

ACT ONE
SCENE 1

The sound of trumpet fanfare. LUCENTIO *and his servant* TRANIO *enter.*

LUCENTIO

Well, Tranio, here we are in fertile Lombardy, garden of Italy, about to fulfill my lifelong dream. You know how I've always longed to see the fair city of Padua, famous for its arts and letters, and now, thanks to my father's generosity, here I am—with his blessing and your good company. So, my trusty servant—and you've never let me down—why don't we settle here for a time to institute a course of study, a really rigorous curriculum. I was born in Pisa, famous for its serious citizens, like my father before me; my father, Vincentio, a successful, world-traveled merchant, was one of the Bentivolii. It's only fitting that I, his son, reared in Florence, should concentrate on adding more virtuous deeds to my father's own, stacking them on top of his wealth. For this reason, Tranio, I'll study ethics and—for the time being, anyway—pursue those areas of philosophy that teach a man how to achieve happiness through virtue. What do you think of all this? Leaving Pisa for Padua, I feel a little like a thirsty man who turns from a puddle to a vast lake he can drink from.

The Bentivolis were one of the leading families of Bologna, wielding great political power and influence.

Lucentio is referring to the philosophy of Aristotle.

Lucentio means he is overwhelmed.

TRANIO

25   *Mi perdonato,* gentle master mine.
    I am in all affected as yourself,
    Glad that you thus continue your resolve
    To suck the sweets of sweet philosophy.
    Only, good master, while we do admire
30   This virtue and this moral discipline,
    Let's be no stoics nor no stocks, I pray,
    Or so devote to Aristotle's checks
    As Ovid be an outcast quite abjured.
    Balk logic with acquaintance that you have,
35   And practice rhetoric in your common talk;
    Music and poesy use to quicken you;
    The mathematics and the metaphysics—
    Fall to them as you find your stomach serves you.
    No profit grows where is no pleasure ta'en.
40   In brief, sir, study what you most affect.

LUCENTIO

    Gramercies, Tranio, well dost thou advise.
    If, Biondello, thou wert come ashore,
    We could at once put us in readiness
    And take a lodging fit to entertain
45   Such friends as time in Padua shall beget.
    But stay awhile. What company is this?

TRANIO

    Master, some show to welcome us to town.

    LUCENTIO *and* TRANIO *stand by*

    Enter BAPTISTA, KATHERINE, BIANCA, GREMIO, *and*
    HORTENSIO

TRANIO

Pardon me, gentle master. As usual, I'm in complete agreement with you about everything, and glad that you still relish the idea of studying philosophy—and let me add that I admire your virtue and your moral discipline. That said, let's not become total stoics or unfeeling blocks of wood and give up all thought of pleasure. We don't want to become so focused on Aristotle that we forget to read Ovid. Here's my thought: practice your logic as you chat with your friends, and your rhetoric in ordinary conversation. Use music and poetry to excite your senses. Math and metaphysics—well, I'd play them by ear, spending only as much time on them as you can stand. There's nothing to be gained from things we take no pleasure in. What I'm saying, sir, is this: study what you most enjoy.

Stoics were ancient Greek philosophers who advocated indifference to pain or pleasure.

Aristotle's writings would have been central to the university curriculum. In contrast, the poet Ovid wrote frequently about erotic love, and much of his work was considered scandalous.

LUCENTIO

Thanks, Tranio. That's good advice. Now if only Biondello would get here, we could find a nice place to stay where the friends we'll make here in Padua could visit us. Wait! Who are all these people?

TRANIO

Maybe it's a parade to welcome us to town, master.

LUCENTIO *and* TRANIO *stand off to one side.*

BAPTISTA *enters with his elder daughter,* KATHERINE, *the younger daughter,* BIANCA, *and two suitors to* BIANCA, *an old man named* GREMIO *and a younger man named* HORTENSIO.

BAPTISTA

Gentlemen, importune me no farther,
For how I firmly am resolved you know—
50 That is, not to bestow my youngest daughter
Before I have a husband for the elder.
If either of you both love Katherina,
Because I know you well and love you well
Leave shall you have to court her at your pleasure.

GREMIO

55 To cart her, rather. She's too rough for me.—
There, there, Hortensio, will you any wife?

KATHERINE

(to BAPTISTA*)* I pray you, sir, is it your will
To make a stale of me amongst these mates?

HORTENSIO

"Mates," maid? how mean you that? No mates for you
60 Unless you were of gentler, milder mold.

KATHERINE

I' faith, sir, you shall never need to fear.
I wis it is not halfway to her heart.
But if it were, doubt not her care should be
To comb your noddle with a three-legged stool
65 And paint your face and use you like a fool.

HORTENSIO

From all such devils, good Lord, deliver us!

GREMIO

And me too, good Lord!

TRANIO

(aside to LUCENTIO*)*
Husht, master, here's some good pastime toward.
That wench is stark mad or wonderful froward.

BAPTISTA

Enough, gentlemen! You can't influence me on this point. You know how I feel. I'm determined not to permit my younger daughter to marry until I have a husband for the elder one. I've long regarded you both as good friends. Therefore, if either of you is partial to Katherina, he shall have my permission to court her freely.

GREMIO

Gremio refers to an Elizabethan practice in which prostitutes and women who were seen as "scolds" were tied behind a cart and whipped as it moved through town.

Cart her, you mean. She's too much for me. How about you, Hortensio? Are you still interested in marrying?

KATHERINE

(to BAPTISTA) May I ask, sir, if it's your intention to publicly humiliate me, showing me off like a whore in front of these suitors?

HORTENSIO

We're not your suitors, that's for sure! Not until you improve your temper, girl!

KATHERINE

Don't worry, I couldn't care less. The only possible interest I could take in you would be to hit you on the head with a stool, paint your face with blood, and make a fool out of you.

HORTENSIO

May the good Lord keep me safe from all women like her!

GREMIO

Me too, Lord!

TRANIO

(speaking so that only LUCENTIO can hear) Wow! This'll be fun to watch! This girl is either completely crazy or incredibly willful.

LUCENTIO

70   *(aside to* TRANIO*)* But in the other's silence do I see
            Maid's mild behavior and sobriety.
            Peace, Tranio.

TRANIO

            (aside to LUCENTIO*)* Well said, master. Mum, and gaze your
            fill.

BAPTISTA

            (to GREMIO *and* HORTENSIO*)*
75   Gentlemen, that I may soon make good
            What I have said—Bianca, get you in,
            And let it not displease thee, good Bianca,
            For I will love thee ne'er the less, my girl.

KATHERINE

            A pretty peat! It is best
80   Put finger in the eye, an she knew why.

BIANCA

            Sister, content you in my discontent.—
            Sir, to your pleasure humbly I subscribe.
            My books and instruments shall be my company,
            On them to look and practice by myself.

LUCENTIO

85   Hark, Tranio! Thou may'st hear Minerva speak.

HORTENSIO

            Signior Baptista, will you be so strange?
            Sorry am I that our goodwill effects
            Bianca's grief.

GREMIO

            Why will you mew her up,
90   Signior Baptista, for this fiend of hell
            And make her bear the penance of her tongue?

LUCENTIO

(speaking so that only TRANIO can hear) But her sister seems quiet and well behaved, as a young girl should be. Shhh, Tranio.

TRANIO

(speaking so that only LUCENTIO can hear) Indeed, master. Let's keep quiet and watch.

BAPTISTA

(to GREMIO and HORTENSIO) Gentlemen, since I'd like to make good on what I've said—Bianca, go inside. And don't be unhappy, my dear. Whatever happens, you know I'll never love you less.

KATHERINE

What a spoiled little brat. She'd make herself cry now, if she could think of a reason.

BIANCA

Sister, be happy in my unhappiness.—Sir, I will humbly obey you. I'll take comfort in my books and music, reading and practicing my instruments.

LUCENTIO

Minerva was the Roman goddess of wisdom. (In Greek mythology, she is called Athena.)

Listen Tranio! That's Minerva's voice you hear.

HORTENSIO

Signior Baptista, will you really be this cruel? I regret that our goodwill should cause Bianca unhappiness.

GREMIO

Why are you locking her away because of this fiend from hell, Signor Baptista? Why does the one daughter have to be punished for the other's mouth?

BAPTISTA
> Gentlemen, content ye. I am resolved.—
> Go in, Bianca.

Exit BIANCA

> And for I know she taketh most delight
> In music, instruments, and poetry,
> Schoolmasters will I keep within my house,
> Fit to instruct her youth. If you, Hortensio,
> Or, Signior Gremio, you know any such,
> Prefer them hither, for to cunning men
> I will be very kind, and liberal
> To mine own children in good bringing up.
> And so farewell.—Katherina, you may stay,
> For I have more to commune with Bianca.

Exit

KATHERINE
> Why, and I trust I may go too, may I not? What, shall I be
> appointed hours as though, belike, I knew not what to take
> and what to leave, ha?

Exit

GREMIO
> You may go to the devil's dam! Your gifts are so good here's
> none will hold you.—Their love is not so great, Hortensio,
> but we may blow our nails together and fast it fairly out.
> Our cake's dough on both sides. Farewell. Yet for the love I
> bear my sweet Bianca, if I can by any means light on a fit
> man to teach her that wherein she delights, I will wish him
> to her father.

BAPTISTA

Gentlemen, I've made my decision. That's all there is to it. Go inside, Bianca.

BIANCA exits.

And because I know how fond she is of music, playing her instruments, and poetry, I plan to hire live-in tutors for her. If either of you gentlemen knows anyone who would be suitable for the job, send him to me. I'll pay well for good teachers. I don't stint when it comes to educating my children. Goodbye, gentlemen. Katherina, you may stay. I have things to discuss with Bianca.

He exits.

KATHERINE

Stay out here? I don't think so! Am I to be dictated to, like a child? Told when to come and where to go? No.

She exits.

GREMIO

You can go straight to hell! What you have to offer is nothing anyone wants. Hortensio, our desire to be married isn't so great that we can't wait this out patiently. It's tough on both of us, but I guess we'll live. So long. But to prove my love for Bianca, I'm going to see if I can find a good tutor to give her lessons in the things she enjoys. If I do, I'll send him to her father.

HORTENSIO

115 So will I, Signior Gremio. But a word, I pray. Though the nature of our quarrel yet never brooked parle, know now upon advice, it toucheth us both, that we may yet again have access to our fair mistress and be happy rivals in Bianca's love, to labor and effect one thing specially.

GREMIO

What's that, I pray?

HORTENSIO

120 Marry, sir, to get a husband for her sister.

GREMIO

A husband? A devil!

HORTENSIO

I say a husband.

GREMIO

I say a devil. Think'st thou, Hortensio, though her father be very rich, any man is so very a fool to be married to hell?

HORTENSIO

125 Tush, Gremio. Though it pass your patience and mine to endure her loud alarums, why, man, there be good fellows in the world, an a man could light on them, would take her with all faults, and money enough.

GREMIO

I cannot tell. But I had as lief take her dowry with this
130 condition: to be whipped at the high cross every morning.

HORTENSIO

Faith, as you say, there's small choice in rotten apples. But come, since this bar in law makes us friends, it shall be so far forth friendly maintained till by helping Baptista's eldest daughter to a husband we set his youngest free for a
135 husband, and then have to 't afresh. Sweet Bianca! Happy man be his dole! He that runs fastest gets the ring. How say you, Signior Gremio?

HORTENSIO

I'll do the same. But wait—don't go just yet, Signior Gremio. I know we've never exactly been allies, but it might be in both our interests, if you think about it, to put our heads together about one particular thing. That is, if we ever want to return to being rivals for Bianca's love.

GREMIO

And that would be—?

HORTENSIO

To find a husband for her sister.

GREMIO

A husband? You mean a devil!

HORTENSIO

I mean a husband.

GREMIO

I say a devil. Do you really think there's a man fool enough to marry into hell—however rich the father is?

HORTENSIO

Oh, I don't know. Just because we wouldn't want to put up with her tantrums, that doesn't mean there aren't guys who would, if we could find them. Guys who'd take her with all her faults, provided there were enough money involved.

GREMIO

I don't know. All I know is *I'd* rather endure a public whipping every morning than put up with her—even with a big dowry.

HORTENSIO

The two choices are about equal, it's true. But come, since we must be friends in the face of this new obstacle, let's work together to find a husband for Baptista's elder daughter, and thus free his younger daughter to have a husband, too. Then we can go back to fighting with each other. Happy the man that claims you, sweet Bianca! And may the best man win. What do you say, Signior Gremio?

GREMIO

I am agreed, and would I had given him the best horse in
Padua to begin his wooing that would thoroughly woo her,
140   wed her, and bed her, and rid the house of her! Come on.

Exeunt GREMIO *and* HORTENSIO

TRANIO

I pray, sir, tell me, is it possible
That love should of a sudden take such hold?

LUCENTIO

O Tranio, till I found it to be true,
I never thought it possible or likely.
145   But see, while idly I stood looking on,
I found the effect of love in idleness
And now in plainness do confess to thee
That art to me as secret and as dear
As Anna to the Queen of Carthage was,
150   Tranio, I burn, I pine, I perish, Tranio,
If I achieve not this young modest girl.
Counsel me, Tranio, for I know thou canst.
Assist me, Tranio, for I know thou wilt.

TRANIO

Master, it is no time to chide you now.
155   Affection is not rated from the heart.
If love have touched you, naught remains but so:
Redime te captum quam queas minimo.

LUCENTIO

Gramercies, lad, go forward. This contents.
The rest will comfort, for thy counsel's sound.

TRANIO

160   Master, you looked so longly on the maid,
Perhaps you marked not what's the pith of all.

GREMIO

Agreed. This imaginary suitor for Katherina—I'd buy him the best horse in Padua if he'd get here quickly, woo her, marry her, take her to bed, and rid the house of her. Let's go.

GREMIO and HORTENSIO *exit.*

TRANIO

Sir, is it possible that a person could fall in love so suddenly?

LUCENTIO

Oh, Tranio, until it happened to me, I never would have thought it possible. But now I confess it openly to you, Tranio. You are to me what Anna, Dido's sister, was to the Queen of Carthage. I confide in you. I tell you, Tranio, I'm on fire, in agony. I'll die if I can't have this modest young girl for my wife. Advise me, Tranio—I know you can. Help me, Tranio—I know you will.

In Virgil's Aeneid, *Dido, queen of Carthage, confessed her secret passion for Aeneas to her sister, Anna.*

TRANIO

Master, this is no moment to lecture you. The heart won't be reasoned with. If love has touched you, love has touched you—end of story. But, as the Roman Terence advises, now that you're a captive, it's time to buy back your freedom at the lowest possible cost.

LUCENTIO

Yes, you're right. Please go on. I feel better already, and I know there's more good advice where that came from.

TRANIO

Master, you were so focused on the girl herself, I wonder if you missed the main point here.

LUCENTIO
Oh yes, I saw sweet beauty in her face
Such as the daughter of Agenor had,
That made great Jove to humble him to her hand
165   When with his knees he kissed the Cretan strand.

TRANIO
Saw you no more? Marked you not how her sister
Began to scold and raise up such a storm
That mortal ears might hardly endure the din?

LUCENTIO
Tranio, I saw her coral lips to move
170   And with her breath she did perfume the air.
Sacred and sweet was all I saw in her.

TRANIO
(aside) Nay, then, 'tis time to stir him from his trance.—
I pray, awake, sir! If you love the maid,
Bend thoughts and wits to achieve her. Thus it stands:
175   Her eldest sister is so curst and shrewd
That till the father rid his hands of her,
Master, your love must live a maid at home,
And therefore has he closely mewed her up,
Because she will not be annoyed with suitors.

LUCENTIO
180   Ah, Tranio, what a cruel father's he!
But art thou not advised, he took some care
To get her cunning schoolmasters to instruct her?

TRANIO
Ay, marry, am I, sir; and now 'tis plotted!

LUCENTIO
I have it, Tranio!

TRANIO
                    Master, for my hand,
185   Both our inventions meet and jump in one.

LUCENTIO

Jove, or Zeus, king of the gods, fell in love with Europa, a mortal maiden, and changed himself into a bull, carrying Europa across the sea to Crete, where he raped her.

Oh no! I saw sweetness and beauty in her face of the kind that humbled great Jove. He saw it in Europa that time she brought him to his knees in Crete.

TRANIO

That's all you noticed? You missed the part where her sister began to scold her and made such a ruckus that human ears could hardly stand it?

LUCENTIO

Tranio, I saw her coral-pink lips move and perfume the air with her breath. I saw nothing in her except what is virtuous and lovely.

TRANIO

(to the audience) I think it's time to rouse him from his trance.—Wake up, sir! If you love the girl, it's time to figure out how to win her. The way things stand, her older sister is so bitchy and difficult that the father can't wait to get rid of her. But until he does, your sweetheart is grounded, locked up at home and not allowed any suitors.

LUCENTIO

Oh, Tranio, what a cruel father he is. Still, did you notice how ready he was to hire good tutors for her?

TRANIO

I did—and now I've got it!

LUCENTIO

Tranio, I think I've got it!

TRANIO

I'll bet we're both thinking the same thing, master.

LUCENTIO
Tell me thine first.

TRANIO
You will be schoolmaster
And undertake the teaching of the maid:
That's your device.

LUCENTIO
It is. May it be done?

TRANIO
Not possible. For who shall bear your part
190   And be in Padua here Vincentio's son,
Keep house and ply his book, welcome his friends,
Visit his countrymen and banquet them?

LUCENTIO
Basta, content thee, for I have it full.
We have not yet been seen in any house,
195   Nor can we be distinguished by our faces
For man or master. Then it follows thus:
Thou shalt be master, Tranio, in my stead,
Keep house and port and servants as I should.
I will some other be, some Florentine,
200   Some Neapolitan, or meaner man of Pisa.
'Tis hatched, and shall be so. Tranio, at once
Uncase thee. Take my colored hat and cloak.

They exchange clothes

When Biondello comes, he waits on thee,
But I will charm him first to keep his tongue.

LUCENTIO

Tell me your idea first.

TRANIO

You will pretend to be a schoolmaster and offer to teach the girl. Is that your plan?

LUCENTIO

It is. Do you think it would work?

TRANIO

No, not a chance. You're supposed to be here in Padua studying. So who would fill in for you—pretend to be Vincentio's son, live in his house, pore over his books, welcome his friends, and wine and dine his fellow expatriates from Pisa?

LUCENTIO

Enough! Don't worry, I have it all figured out. No one has seen us yet, and no one knows what we look like— which of us is master and which servant. It's obvious: *You* will be *me,* Tranio—live in my house, instruct the servants and do everything in my place just as I would. I, meanwhile, will impersonate some other made-up fellow—some guy from Florence or Naples, or some poor guy from Pisa. There! That's a plan. Take off what you're wearing and put on my hat and cloak.

They exchange clothes.

When Biondello comes, he'll pretend to be your servant, but I'd better figure out some way to keep him quiet about this.

TRANIO
205   So had you need.
        In brief, sir, sith it your pleasure is,
        And I am tied to be obedient,
        For so your father charged me at our parting,
        "Be serviceable to my son," quoth he,
210   Although I think 'twas in another sense,
        I am content to be Lucentio,
        Because so well I love Lucentio.

LUCENTIO
        Tranio, be so, because Lucentio loves,
        And let me be a slave t'achieve that maid
215   Whose sudden sight hath thralled my wounded eye.

        Enter BIONDELLO

        Here comes the rogue.—Sirrah, where have you been?

BIONDELLO
        Where have I been? Nay, how now, where are you? Master,
        has my fellow Tranio stolen your clothes? Or you stolen
        his? Or both? Pray, what's the news?

LUCENTIO
220   Sirrah, come hither: 'tis no time to jest,
        And therefore frame your manners to the time.
        Your fellow Tranio here, to save my life,
        Puts my apparel and my countenance on,
        And I for my escape have put on his;
225   For in a quarrel since I came ashore
        I killed a man and fear I was descried.
        Wait you on him, I charge you, as becomes,
        While I make way from hence to save my life.
        You understand me?

BIONDELLO
                        Aye, sir. *(aside)* Ne'er a whit.

TRANIO

Yeah, you'd better. Meanwhile, since this is how you want to play it, I must obey. Because, you know, your father expressly told me before we left, "Make yourself useful to my son"—though I don't think he had this in mind. I am happy to *become* Lucentio because I love him so much.

LUCENTIO

Good, because Lucentio is also in love. I will enslave myself to win the girl whose beauty has enslaved me.

BIONDELLO *enters.*

Here comes Biondello. Where have you been, boy?

BIONDELLO

Where have *I* been? Where are *you?* Has Tranio stolen your clothes, master? Or have you stolen his? Have you both stolen each other's? Please, what's going on?

LUCENTIO

Come here, boy. It's no time for jokes: sober up. Tranio and I have traded clothes to save my life. I killed a man in a fight since we came ashore, and I'm worried someone saw me. While I make my escape, I need you to wait on Tranio as though he were me. Understand?

BIONDELLO

Of course, sir. *(to the audience)* Not a word.

LUCENTIO

230   And not a jot of "Tranio" in your mouth.
        Tranio is changed into Lucentio.

BIONDELLO

        The better for him. Would I were so too.

TRANIO

        So could I, faith, boy, to have the next wish after,
        That Lucentio indeed had Baptista's youngest daughter.
235   But, sirrah, not for my sake, but your master's, I advise
        You use your manners discreetly in all kind of companies.
        When I am alone, why then I am Tranio;
        But in all places else, your master Lucentio.

LUCENTIO

        Tranio, let's go. One thing more rests, that thyself execute,
240   to make one among these wooers. If thou ask me why,
        sufficeth my reasons are both good and weighty.

Exeunt

The presenters above speak

FIRST SERVANT

        My lord, you nod. You do not mind the play.

SLY

        Yes, by Saint Anne, do I. A good matter, surely. Comes
        there any more of it?

PAGE

245   My lord, 'tis but begun.

SLY

        'Tis a very excellent piece of work, madam lady. Would
        'twere done.

They sit and mark

LUCENTIO

And you're not to utter a syllable of Tranio's name. "Tranio" is now "Lucentio."

BIONDELLO

Lucky for him. Wish I could say the same.

TRANIO

I'd second your wish if it automatically meant that Lucentio could have Baptista's youngest daughter. This is for your master's sake, not mine. So watch your step when there are other people around. When we're by ourselves you can call me "Tranio." Everywhere else, address me as your master Lucentio.

LUCENTIO

Tranio, let's go. One last thing, and this is up to you. You'll have to woo Bianca like the rest. Don't ask why. Just trust me—I know what I'm doing.

They exit.

The presenters up in the balcony speak.

FIRST SERVANT

(to SLY*)* My lord, you're falling asleep. You're not paying attention to the play.

SLY

No, no. I am. Really. Very impressive. Is there any more, or is that it?

PAGE

(speaking as SLY*'s wife)* My lord, we've only just got started.

SLY

And what an excellent piece of work it is, too, madam lady! I wish it were over.

They sit and watch.

ACT 1, SCENE 2

Enter PETRUCHIO *and his man* GRUMIO

PETRUCHIO
Verona, for a while I take my leave,
To see my friends in Padua, but of all
My best belovèd and approvèd friend,
Hortensio. And I trow this is his house.
5   Here, sirrah Grumio. Knock, I say.

GRUMIO
Knock, sir? Whom should I knock? Is there any man has
rebused your Worship?

PETRUCHIO
Villain, I say, knock me here soundly.

GRUMIO
Knock you here, sir? Why, sir, what am I, sir, that I should
10   knock you here, sir?

PETRUCHIO
Villain, I say, knock me at this gate
And rap me well, or I'll knock your knave's pate.

GRUMIO
My master is grown quarrelsome. I should knock you first,
And then I know after who comes by the worst.

PETRUCHIO
15   Will it not be?
Faith, sirrah, an you'll not knock, I'll ring it.
I'll try how you can *sol, fa,* and sing it.

He wrings him by the ears

GRUMIO
Help, mistress, help! My master is mad.

ACT 1, SCENE 2

PETRUCHIO *enters with his servant* GRUMIO.

PETRUCHIO

Farewell, Verona! I'm off to visit my friends in Padua—particularly my best friend Hortensio. And I think this is his house. Here, you there, Grumio. Knock.

GRUMIO

Knock, sir? Whom should I knock? Has anyone offended your Worship?

PETRUCHIO

Moron! I'm telling you to make a fist and pound.

GRUMIO

Grumio acts as if Petruchio asked Grumio to hit him.

Really, sir, I hardly think it would be appropriate for me to pound you.

PETRUCHIO

Moron, here we are at the gate. Now put your fists to work, or I'll put mine to work on your head!

GRUMIO

My master is being difficult. If I do as he asks I think I know which one of us will be sorrier—and it's not going to be him!

PETRUCHIO

What are you standing there for! If you won't knock, I'll ring—and you'll be singing along in falsetto!

He grabs him by the ears.

GRUMIO

(to the unseen mistress or master of the house) Help, mistress, help! My master has gone mad.

PETRUCHIO
> Now knock when I bid you, sirrah villain.

Enter HORTENSIO

HORTENSIO
20 > How now, what's the matter? My old friend Grumio and
> my good friend Petruchio? How do you all at Verona?

PETRUCHIO
> Signior Hortensio, come you to part the fray?
> *Con tutto il cuore, ben trovato,* may I say.

HORTENSIO
> Alla nostra casa ben venuto, molto honorato signor mio
25 > Petruchio.—Rise, Grumio, rise. We will compound this
> quarrel.

GRUMIO
> Nay, 'tis no matter, sir, what he 'leges in Latin. If this be not
> a lawful case for me to leave his service—look you, sir: he
> bid me knock him and rap him soundly, sir. Well, was it fit
30 > for a servant to use his master so, being perhaps, for aught
> I see, two-and-thirty, a pip out?
> Whom, would to God, I had well knocked at first,
> Then had not Grumio come by the worst.

PETRUCHIO
> A senseless villain, good Hortensio.
35 > I bade the rascal knock upon your gate
> And could not get him for my heart to do it.

GRUMIO
> Knock at the gate? O heavens! Spake you not these words
> plain: "Sirrah, knock me here, rap me here, knock me well,
> and knock me soundly"? And come you now with
40 > "knocking at the gate"?

PETRUCHIO
> Sirrah, begone or talk not, I advise you.

PETRUCHIO

Next time maybe you'll knock when I tell you, punk kid!

HORTENSIO *enters.*

HORTENSIO

Say, what's the trouble? If it isn't my old friend Grumio—and my dear friend Petruchio! How's everyone in Verona?

PETRUCHIO

The Italian means, "With all my heart, I'm glad to see you."

Hortensio, have you come to break up the fight? *Con tutto il cuore ben trovato,* if I may say so.

HORTENSIO

The Italian means, "You are welcome here, my most honored Signior Petruchio!"

Alla nostra casa ben venuto, molto honorato signor mio Petruchio! Get up, Grumio. We'll settle this quarrel.

GRUMIO

I don't care what he told you in Latin. If this isn't legal justification for me to leave his service, I don't know what is. He tells me to knock him, pound him, and put my fists to work on him. Well, I ask you, was that any way for a servant to behave toward his master—especially when he's clearly a bit crazy. I wish I *had* hit him. I think I'd feel a lot better.

PETRUCHIO

He's a worthless dog, Hortensio. I told him to knock at your gate and for the life of me could not get him to do it.

GRUMIO

Knock at the gate? Oh, for Pete's sake! Didn't you clearly say "Knock," "pound," and "put your fists to work"? Now you say it was "Knock at the gate"?

PETRUCHIO

Grumio, either leave or shut up. I'm warning you.

HORTENSIO
Petruchio, patience. I am Grumio's pledge.
Why, this' a heavy chance 'twixt him and you,
Your ancient, trusty, pleasant servant Grumio.
45   And tell me now, sweet friend, what happy gale
Blows you to Padua here from old Verona?

PETRUCHIO
Such wind as scatters young men through the world
To seek their fortunes farther than at home,
Where small experience grows. But in a few,
50   Signior Hortensio, thus it stands with me:
Antonio, my father, is deceased,
And I have thrust myself into this maze,
Happily to wive and thrive as best I may.
Crowns in my purse I have and goods at home,
55   And so am come abroad to see the world.

HORTENSIO
Petruchio, shall I then come roundly to thee
And wish thee to a shrewd, ill-favored wife?
Thou'dst thank me but a little for my counsel;
And yet I'll promise thee she shall be rich,
60   And very rich. But thou'rt too much my friend,
And I'll not wish thee to her.

PETRUCHIO
Signior Hortensio, 'twixt such friends as we
Few words suffice. And therefore, if thou know
One rich enough to be Petruchio's wife,
65   As wealth is burden of my wooing dance,
Be she as foul as was Florentius' love,
As old as Sibyl and as curst and shrewd
As Socrates' Xanthippe, or a worse,
She moves me not, or not removes at least
70   Affection's edge in me, were she as rough
As are the swelling Adriatic seas.
I come to wive it wealthily in Padua;
If wealthily, then happily in Padua.

HORTENSIO

Easy, Petruchio. I'll vouch for Grumio. It's terrible—
you two fighting! Faithful, funny old Grumio! You
guys go way back! Now, my dear friend, what lucky
wind blows you in from Verona?

PETRUCHIO

The wind that scatters young men throughout the
world, encouraging them to seek their fortunes some
place other than home, where there's little to be found
in the way of experience. But to be brief, Hortensio,
the situation is that my father, Antonio, is dead, and I
have set off into this crazy world to see if I can marry
well and make a good life for myself. I have money in
my purse and property at home, so I'm off to see the
world.

HORTENSIO

Petruchio, shall I be frank? I know where you can find
a shrewish and unpleasant wife. I doubt you'd thank
me in the end, but she's rich, all right, very rich. But
you're too good a friend for me to wish her on you.

PETRUCHIO

Hortensio, good friends like us can get by on a few
words. If you can find a woman rich enough for me—
because money is all I look for in a wife—let her be as
ugly as Florentius's love, as old as the Sibyl, and as
bad-tempered as Xanthippe. It wouldn't matter one
way or the other. I've come here in search of a rich
wife. If I find a rich wife in Padua, I'll have found a
good wife in Padua.

*Florentius was a
knight in a medi-
eval poem by John
Gower; he was
forced to marry an
extremely ugly
woman. The
Cumaean Sibyl was
a mythical proph-
etess who lived
forever. Xanthippe
was Socrates'
notoriously bad-
tempered wife.*

GRUMIO

(*to* HORTENSIO) Nay, look you, sir, he tells you flatly what
75　　his mind is. Why, give him gold enough and marry him to
a puppet or an aglet-baby, or an old trot with ne'er a tooth
in her head, though she have as many diseases as two-and-
fifty horses. Why, nothing comes amiss, so money comes
withal.

HORTENSIO

80　　Petruchio, since we are stepped thus far in,
I will continue that I broached in jest.
I can, Petruchio, help thee to a wife
With wealth enough, and young and beauteous,
Brought up as best becomes a gentlewoman.
85　　Her only fault, and that is faults enough,
Is that she is intolerable curst,
And shrewd and froward, so beyond all measure
That, were my state far worser than it is,
I would not wed her for a mine of gold.

PETRUCHIO

90　　Hortensio, peace. Thou know'st not gold's effect.
Tell me her father's name, and 'tis enough;
For I will board her, though she chide as loud
As thunder when the clouds in autumn crack.

HORTENSIO

Her father is Baptista Minola,
95　　An affable and courteous gentleman.
Her name is Katherina Minola,
Renowned in Padua for her scolding tongue.

PETRUCHIO

I know her father, though I know not her,
And he knew my deceasèd father well.
100　　I will not sleep, Hortensio, till I see her,
And therefore let me be thus bold with you
To give you over at this first encounter,
Unless you will accompany me thither.

GRUMIO

> (*to* HORTENSIO) He's certainly frank, isn't he, sir? Give him enough money and he'll be happy with a puppet, a paper doll, or a diseased old hag without a tooth in her head. If she's got money, what does it matter?

HORTENSIO

> Petruchio, since the conversation's gone this far, I may as well carry on with what I mentioned purely as a joke. I can help you find a wife who's rich, young, beautiful, and reared in a manner fit for a gentlewoman. Her only flaw—and it's a big one—is that she's unbearable, a total witch, so much so that I wouldn't think of marrying her myself, not even if I were in a worse fix than I am, not for a whole goldmine.

PETRUCHIO

> Hush, Hortensio. You don't know what money can buy. Tell me her father's name—that's all I need. I will go after her even if her scolding is as deafening as thunder in an autumn rainstorm.

HORTENSIO

> Her father is Baptista Minola, a pleasant and courteous gentleman. Her name is Katherina Minola, famous throughout Padua for her scolding tongue.

PETRUCHIO

> I don't know her, but I know her father and he knew mine well. I won't sleep until I see her, Hortensio. So I hope you'll forgive my cutting short this first conversation of ours—unless you want to come with me.

GRUMIO

(to HORTENSIO*)* I pray you, sir, let him go while the humor
105 lasts. O' my word, an she knew him as well as I do, she
would think scolding would do little good upon him. She
may perhaps call him half a score knaves or so. Why, that's
nothing; an he begin once, he'll rail in his rope tricks. I'll tell
you what sir: an she stand him but a little, he will throw a
110 figure in her face and so disfigure her with it that she shall
have no more eyes to see withal than a cat. You know him
not, sir.

HORTENSIO

Tarry, Petruchio, I must go with thee,
For in Baptista's keep my treasure is.
115 He hath the jewel of my life in hold,
His youngest daughter, beautiful Bianca,
And her withholds from me and other more,
Suitors to her and rivals in my love,
Supposing it a thing impossible,
120 For those defects I have before rehearsed,
That ever Katherina will be wooed.
Therefore this order hath Baptista ta'en,
That none shall have access unto Bianca
Till Katherine the curst have got a husband.

GRUMIO

125 "Katherine the curst!"
A title for a maid of all titles the worst.

HORTENSIO

Now shall my friend Petruchio do me grace,
And offer me disguised in sober robes
To old Baptista as a schoolmaster
130 Well seen in music, to instruct Bianca,
That so I may, by this device at least,
Have leave and leisure to make love to her
And, unsuspected, court her by herself.

GRUMIO

> *(to* HORTENSIO*)* Please, sir, let him go while he's in this mood. Lord! If she knew him as well as I do, she'd realize how little effect a scolding has on him. At best she may come up with nine or ten abusive things to call him. That's nothing. Once he starts on her, he'll rant and rave on an epic scale. In fact, if she even tries to face him down, he'll throw out a figure of speech that so disfigures her she'll have no more eyes to see with than a cat. You don't know him, sir.

HORTENSIO

> Wait, Petruchio, I should go with you. My own "wealth" is in Baptista's keeping. His youngest daughter, the beautiful Bianca, is the jewel of my life, and he keeps her hidden away from me and other rivals for her hand. Because he finds it so incredible—owing to those character deficiencies I mentioned before—that any man will ever come courting Katherina, Baptista has therefore issued this edict: that none shall be permitted to court Bianca until that Katherine the shrew finds a husband.

GRUMIO

> "Katherine the shrew!" That's the worst thing you can call a young woman.

HORTENSIO

> Now my friend Petruchio will help me out, presenting me to old Baptista as a schoolmaster for Bianca well-versed in music. I'll disguise myself in somber robes. In this costume, I'll be able to spend time with her alone, which will give me plenty of opportunity to court her.

GRUMIO

135   Here's no knavery! See, to beguile the old folks, how the
        young folks lay their heads together!

Enter GREMIO *and* LUCENTIO *disguised as* CAMBIO

        Master, master, look about you. Who goes there, ha?

HORTENSIO

        Peace, Grumio. It is the rival of my love.
        Petruchio, stand by a while.

PETRUCHIO, HORTENSIO, *and* GRUMIO *stand aside*

GRUMIO

        (aside) A proper stripling, and an amorous.

GREMIO

140   *(to* LUCENTIO*)* O, very well, I have perused the note.
        Hark you, sir: I'll have them very fairly bound,
        All books of love. See that at any hand,
        And see you read no other lectures to her.
        You understand me. Over and beside
145   Signior Baptista's liberality,
        I'll mend it with a largess. Take your paper too.
        And let me have them very well perfum'd
        For she is sweeter than perfume itself
        To whom they go to. What will you read to her?

LUCENTIO

150   *(as* CAMBIO*)* Whate'er I read to her, I'll plead for you
        As for my patron, stand you so assured,
        As firmly as yourself were still in place,
        Yea, and perhaps with more successful words
        Than you, unless you were a scholar, sir.

GREMIO

155   O this learning, what a thing it is!

GRUMIO

> Oh, *very* nice! See how the young folks conspire to fool the old folks!

> GREMIO *enters with* LUCENTIO, *disguised as* CAMBIO.

> Master, master, look! Who are these people?

HORTENSIO

> Hush, Grumio. It is my rival for Bianca. Petruchio, let's stand over here awhile.

> PETRUCHIO, HORTENSIO, *and* GRUMIO *stand off to the side.*

GRUMIO

> *(to the audience, indicating old* GREMIO*)* Check out this stud! What a heartthrob!

GREMIO

> *(to* LUCENTIO*)* Oh, all right, I've reviewed the list of books. But listen: I want them very handsomely bound—only books of love, make sure of that in any case. And see that you give her no other lessons. Do I make myself clear? Over and above what Signior Baptista pays you, I'll tack on a bonus. Take these notes, too. And make sure they're pleasantly perfumed. The lady they are meant for is sweeter than perfume itself. What are you planning to read her?

LUCENTIO

> *(speaking as* CAMBIO*)* Whatever I read her, you can be sure that I'll plead the case for your love as strongly as if you yourself stood there before her—and perhaps even a bit more successfully than you would do, sir, seeing as you're not a scholar.

GREMIO

> Oh, what an excellent thing this learning is!

GRUMIO
> *(aside)* O this woodcock, what an ass it is!

PETRUCHIO
> *(aside)* Peace, sirrah!

HORTENSIO
> *(aside)* Grumio, mum! God save you, Signior Gremio.

GREMIO
> And you are well met, Signior Hortensio.
160 | Trow you whither I am going? To Baptista Minola.
> I promised to enquire carefully
> About a schoolmaster for the fair Bianca,
> And by good fortune I have lighted well
> On this young man, for learning and behavior
165 | Fit for her turn, well read in poetry
> And other books—good ones, I warrant ye.

HORTENSIO
> 'Tis well. And I have met a gentleman
> Hath promised me to help me to another,
> A fine musician to instruct our mistress.
170 | So shall I no whit be behind in duty
> To fair Bianca, so beloved of me.

GREMIO
> Beloved of me, and that my deeds shall prove.

GRUMIO
> *(aside)* And that his bags shall prove.

HORTENSIO
> Gremio, 'tis now no time to vent our love.
175 | Listen to me, and if you speak me fair,
> I'll tell you news indifferent good for either.

GRUMIO

(speaking to the audience) Oh, what an asinine thing this moron is!

PETRUCHIO

(speaking so that only GRUMIO can hear) Silence, boy!

HORTENSIO

(speaking so that only GRUMIO can hear) Grumio, hush! *(to GREMIO, who can't hear him)* God save you, Signior Gremio.

GREMIO

Good to see you, Signior Hortensio. Do you know where I'm going? To Baptista Minola's house. I promised to look into schoolmasters for Miss Bianca, and luck has led me to this young man, perfectly suited in learning and fine manners, well read in poetry and other books—all of them good, I assure you.

HORTENSIO

That's great. And I have met a gentleman who promises to help me find a good music tutor to instruct our lady love. I wouldn't want to fall behind in my devotion to my beloved Bianca.

GREMIO

My beloved—as my actions will prove.

GRUMIO

(speaking to the audience) As his moneybags will prove.

HORTENSIO

Gremio, this is no time to compete over how deeply we love Bianca. Be nice and listen to me a moment, and I'll give you a piece of news that's equally good for both of us.

(presenting PETRUCHIO*)*
Here is a gentleman whom by chance I met,
Upon agreement from us to his liking,
Will undertake to woo curst Katherine,
180   Yea, and to marry her, if her dowry please.

GREMIO
So said, so done, is well.
Hortensio, have you told him all her faults?

PETRUCHIO
I know she is an irksome brawling scold.
If that be all, masters, I hear no harm.

GREMIO
185   No? Say'st me so, friend? What countryman?

PETRUCHIO
Born in Verona, old Antonio's son.
My father dead, my fortune lives for me.
And I do hope good days and long to see.

GREMIO
O sir, such a life with such a wife were strange!
190   But if you have a stomach, to 't, i' God's name:
You shall have me assisting you in all.
But will you woo this wildcat?

PETRUCHIO
                    Will I live?

GRUMIO
Will he woo her? Ay, or I'll hang her.

PETRUCHIO
Why came I hither but to that intent?
195   Think you a little din can daunt mine ears?
Have I not in my time heard lions roar?
Have I not heard the sea, puffed up with winds,
Rage like an angry boar chafèd with sweat?
Have I not heard great ordnance in the field,
200   And heaven's artillery thunder in the skies?

(presenting PETRUCHIO*)* Here is a gentleman I happened to meet who, if we can come to an arrangement that would be to his liking, is willing to undertake to woo fierce Katherine—yes, even willing to marry her, if the price is right.

GREMIO

That's good, if he'll really do it. Have you told him all her faults, Hortensio?

PETRUCHIO

I know she is a hateful, brawling scold. If that's all, gentlemen, I see no problem.

GREMIO

No? Tell me, friend. Where are you from?

PETRUCHIO

Born in Verona. I'm old Antonio's son. My father's dead, and his fortune is mine now. I hope to see good days—and many of them.

GREMIO

Sir, such a life with such a wife is unlikely! But if you have the stomach for it, you'll have all the help from me you need. Do you really mean to go after this wildcat?

PETRUCHIO

Do I mean to go on breathing?

GRUMIO

He'll woo her or I'll hang her.

PETRUCHIO

Why did I come here if not for that? Do you think a little burst of noise can intimidate me—I, who have heard lions roar? I, who have survived storms at sea where the winds raged like wild animals? I, who have heard the rumble of guns in battle—and thunder in the sky (heaven's version of artillery).

Have I not in a pitchèd battle heard
Loud 'larums, neighing steeds, and trumpets' clang?
And do you tell me of a woman's tongue
That gives not half so great a blow to hear
205   As will a chestnut in a farmer's fire?
Tush, tush! Fear boys with bugs.

GRUMIO
For he fears none.

GREMIO
Hortensio, hark.
This gentleman is happily arrived,
210   My mind presumes, for his own good and ours.

HORTENSIO
I promised we would be contributors
And bear his charge of wooing, whatsoe'er.

GREMIO
And so we will, provided that he win her.

GRUMIO
I would I were as sure of a good dinner.

Enter TRANIO *brave and* BIONDELLO

TRANIO
215   *(as* LUCENTIO*)* Gentlemen, God save you. If I may be bold,
Tell me, I beseech you, which is the readiest way
To the house of Signior Baptista Minola?

BIONDELLO
He that has the two fair daughters—is 't he you mean?

TRANIO
(as LUCENTIO*)* Even he, Biondello.

GREMIO
220   Hark you, sir, you mean not her to—

Have I not stood in the middle of a battle, with loud calls to arms, horses neighing, and trumpets sounding all around me? And you worry how I'll react to a woman's tongue, which isn't even as loud as the *pop!* of a chestnut roasting in some farmer's oven? Please. Scare children with your bugaboos.

GRUMIO

Because he's not afraid of them.

GREMIO

Listen, Hortensio. I think this gentleman's arrival could be most fortunate—both for himself and for us.

HORTENSIO

I promised him that we would all chip in and take care of the wooing expenses, whatever they come to.

GREMIO

Absolutely—so long as he gets the girl.

GRUMIO

I wish I could be as certain of a good dinner.

TRANIO *enters, lavishly dressed in gentlemen's clothes; he is accompanied by* BIONDELLO.

TRANIO

(speaking as LUCENTIO*)* Greetings, gentlemen. May I be so bold as to ask the fastest way to Signior Baptista Minola's house?

BIONDELLO

The old man with the two pretty daughters? Is that the man you want?

TRANIO

(speaking as LUCENTIO*)* The very one, Biondello.

GREMIO

Pardon, sir, I hope you're not looking for the daughter—

TRANIO

(as LUCENTIO*)*
Perhaps him and her, sir. What have you to do?

PETRUCHIO

Not her that chides, sir, at any hand, I pray.

TRANIO

(as LUCENTIO*)* I love no chiders, sir. Biondello, let's away.

LUCENTIO

(aside) Well begun, Tranio.

HORTENSIO

Sir, a word ere you go.
225   Are you a suitor to the maid you talk of, yea or no?

TRANIO

An if I be, sir, is it any offense?

GREMIO

No, if without more words you will get you hence.

TRANIO

(as LUCENTIO*)* Why, sir, I pray, are not the streets as free
For me as for you?

GREMIO

But so is not she.

TRANIO

230   For what reason, I beseech you?

GREMIO

For this reason, if you'll know:
That she's the choice love of Signior Gremio.

HORTENSIO

That she's the chosen of Signior Hortensio.

TRANIO

Softly, my masters. If you be gentlemen,
235   Do me this right: hear me with patience.
Baptista is a noble gentleman,
To whom my father is not all unknown,
And were his daughter fairer than she is,
She may more suitors have, and me for one.

TRANIO

(speaking as LUCENTIO) I might be looking for both the daughter and her father. What's it to you?

PETRUCHIO

But not the woman who scolds, anyway, I hope.

TRANIO

(speaking as LUCENTIO) I'm not a fan of scolds, my friend. Come, Biondello.

LUCENTIO

(speaking quietly) Nice work, Tranio!

HORTENSIO

Sir, a word before you go. Are you a suitor to the girl we speak of, yes or no?

TRANIO

What if I am? Is there a problem?

GREMIO

Not if you go away, there isn't.

TRANIO

(speaking as LUCENTIO) Well, it seems to me that the streets are as much mine as yours.

GREMIO

But she isn't.

TRANIO

And why is that, please?

GREMIO

Because, if you must know, she's been chosen by Signior Gremio.

HORTENSIO

Because she's been chosen by Signior Hortensio.

TRANIO

Wait a minute, gentlemen. Be good enough to hear me out. Baptista is a noble gentleman—one to whom my father is not completely unknown—and lovely as his daughter is, she is entitled to any number of suitors—myself among them.

240   Fair Leda's daughter had a thousand wooers;
Then well one more may fair Bianca have.
And so she shall. Lucentio shall make one,
Though Paris came in hope to speed alone.

GREMIO
     What! This gentleman will out-talk us all.

LUCENTIO
245   *(as* CAMBIO*)* Sir, give him head; I know he'll prove a jade.

PETRUCHIO
     Hortensio, to what end are all these words?

HORTENSIO
     (to TRANIO*)* Sir, let me be so bold as ask you,
Did you yet ever see Baptista's daughter?

TRANIO
     (as LUCENTIO*)* No, sir, but hear I do that he hath two,
250   The one as famous for a scolding tongue
As is the other for beauteous modesty.

PETRUCHIO
     Sir, sir, the first's for me; let her go by.

GREMIO
     Yea, leave that labor to great Hercules,
And let it be more than Alcides' twelve.

PETRUCHIO
255   *(to* TRANIO*)* Sir, understand you this of me, in sooth:
The youngest daughter, whom you hearken for,
Her father keeps from all access of suitors
And will not promise her to any man
Until the elder sister first be wed.
260   The younger then is free, and not before.

The beautiful Helen of Troy had a thousand suitors. Let Bianca have one more—anyway, she's got one. Lucentio shall join the ranks, even if Paris himself comes to woo her.

Paris was the Trojan prince who stole Helen from her Greek husband, starting the Trojan War.

GREMIO

This fellow will out-talk us all.

LUCENTIO

(*speaking as* CAMBIO) Well, let him. He'll talk himself out, soon.

PETRUCHIO

Hortensio, what's all this about?

HORTENSIO

(*to* TRANIO) Forgive me for asking, but have you ever actually seen Baptista's daughter?

TRANIO

(*speaking as* LUCENTIO) No, but I hear he has two, the one as famous for her scolding tongue as the other is for her modesty and beauty.

PETRUCHIO

The first one's mine, so hands off!

GREMIO

Yes, leave that labor to great Hercules—it's worse than the previous twelve put together.

PETRUCHIO

(*to* TRANIO) Sir, let me be clear. As far as the youngest daughter, the one you were asking about, is concerned, the father refuses any suitors access to her. He will not promise her to any man until the elder sister is married. Then and only then will the younger be free to marry.

TRANIO
    (as LUCENTIO*)* If it be so, sir, that you are the man
    Must stead us all, and me amongst the rest,
    And if you break the ice and do this feat,
    Achieve the elder, set the younger free
265   For our access, whose hap shall be to have her
    Will not so graceless be to be ingrate.

HORTENSIO
    Sir, you say well, and well you do conceive.
    And since you do profess to be a suitor,
    You must, as we do, gratify this gentleman,
270   To whom we all rest generally beholding.

TRANIO
    (as LUCENTIO*)* Sir, I shall not be slack; in sign whereof,
    Please ye we may contrive this afternoon
    And quaff carouses to our mistress' health
    And do as adversaries do in law,
275   Strive mightily, but eat and drink as friends.

GRUMIO *AND* **BIONDELLO**
    O excellent motion! Fellows, let's be gone.

HORTENSIO
    The motion's good indeed and be it so.—
    Petruchio, I shall be your *ben venuto.*

                             Exeunt

TRANIO

> (*as* LUCENTIO) If that's the case, then you're the man to help us, me along with the rest. And if you carry it off and break the ice—win the older and make the younger accessible to us—whoever winds up with her will not be such a boor as to be ungrateful, I'm sure.

HORTENSIO

> Sir, that's well said and well thought out. Now, since you count yourself among Bianca's suitors, you must—as we already have—pay this gentlemen to whom we are all so indebted.

TRANIO

> (*speaking as* LUCENTIO) I'll ante up, certainly! And on that note, let's all pass the time this afternoon drinking rounds to our mistress's health and following the example of legal adversaries, who fight tooth and nail in court but eat and drink as friends.

GRUMIO *AND* **BIONDELLO**

> An excellent motion. Let's go.

A motion is a legal maneuver in court.

HORTENSIO

> I second that motion. So be it. Petruchio, I'm buying.

They all exit.

ACT TWO
SCENE 1

Enter KATHERINE *and* BIANCA, *her hands bound*

BIANCA
> Good sister, wrong me not nor wrong yourself,
> To make a bondmaid and a slave of me.
> That I disdain. But for these other goods—
> Unbind my hands, I'll pull them off myself,
5 > Yea, all my raiment to my petticoat,
> Or what you will command me will I do,
> So well I know my duty to my elders.

KATHERINE
> Of all thy suitors here I charge thee tell
> Whom thou lovest best. See thou dissemble not.

BIANCA
10 > Believe me, sister, of all the men alive
> I never yet beheld that special face
> Which I could fancy more than any other.

KATHERINE
> Minion, thou liest. Is 't not Hortensio?

BIANCA
> If you affect him, sister, here I swear
15 > I'll plead for you myself, but you shall have him.

KATHERINE
> Oh, then belike you fancy riches more.
> You will have Gremio to keep you fair.

BIANCA
> Is it for him you do envy me so?
> Nay, then you jest, and now I well perceive
20 > You have but jested with me all this while.
> I prithee, sister Kate, untie my hands.

> KATHERINE *strikes her*

ACT TWO
SCENE 1

KATHERINE *and* BIANCA *enter.* BIANCA*'s hands are tied.*

BIANCA

Dear sister, it's unfair to me—and unfair to yourself—
to turn me into a slave. That I won't stand for. But if
you want my *things*—untie my hands and I'll give
them to you myself, everything, even down to my slip.
Or anything else you order me to do. I know I should
obey my elders.

KATHERINE

What I want is for you to tell me which of your suitors
you like best. And don't lie.

BIANCA

I swear, dear sister, I have not yet encountered that
special face I might prefer to any other.

KATHERINE

You lying brat. It's Hortensio, isn't it?

BIANCA

If you want him, dear sister, he's yours. I swear I'll
woo him for you myself.

KATHERINE

Oh, I see. You're more interested in money. You'll live
in luxury with Gremio.

BIANCA

Is it because of *him* that you envy me? You must be kid-
ding! And now I see that you've been joking all the
while. Please, Kate, untie my hands.

KATHERINE *strikes her.*

KATHERINE
　　　　If that be jest, then all the rest was so.

Enter BAPTISTA

BAPTISTA
　　　　Why, how now, dame! whence grows this insolence?—
　　　　Bianca, stand aside.—Poor girl, she weeps!
25　　　*(to* BIANCA*)* Go ply thy needle; meddle not with her.
　　　　(to KATHERINE*)* For shame, thou hilding of a devilish spirit!
　　　　Why dost thou wrong her that did ne'er wrong thee?
　　　　When did she cross thee with a bitter word?

KATHERINE
　　　　Her silence flouts me, and I'll be revenged.

Flies after BIANCA

BAPTISTA
30　　　What, in my sight?—Bianca, get thee in.

Exit BIANCA

KATHERINE
　　　　What, will you not suffer me? Nay, now I see
　　　　She is your treasure, she must have a husband,
　　　　I must dance barefoot on her wedding day
　　　　And, for your love to her, lead apes in hell.
35　　　Talk not to me. I will go sit and weep
　　　　Till I can find occasion of revenge.

Exit

BAPTISTA
　　　　Was ever gentleman thus grieved as I?
　　　　But who comes here?

KATHERINE

If *that's* a joke, I guess the rest was, too.

BAPTISTA enters.

BAPTISTA

What in the world is going on! *(to KATHERINE)* Young lady, where do you get the nerve!—*(to BIANCA)* Get behind me, Bianca.—Poor girl, she's hysterical!—Go do some sewing. Don't even talk to her. *(to KATHERINE)* You monstrous, good-for-nothing fiend! Why would you want to hurt your sister? She never did you any harm! When has she spoken even one cross word to you?

KATHERINE

She mocks me with her silence, and I'll get my revenge on her.

She runs at BIANCA as if she's going to strike her.

BAPTISTA

What, in my presence? How dare you!—Bianca, go inside.

BIANCA exits.

KATHERINE

You mean you don't even want to hear my side? Of course! She's your treasure. She must have a husband and I must dance barefoot on her wedding day. You like her best and so I'll die an old maid. Don't talk to me. I'll just go cry myself sick and think of some way to get back at all of you.

She exits.

BAPTISTA

Has any man ever had to put up with what I do? Now what?

Enter GREMIO, LUCENTIO *in the habit of a mean man;*
PETRUCHIO, *with* HORTENSIO *as a musician; and* TRANIO,
with BIONDELLO *bearing a lute and books*

GREMIO
> Good morrow, neighbor Baptista.

BAPTISTA
40 > Good morrow, neighbor Gremio.—God save you,
> gentlemen!

PETRUCHIO
> And you, good sir. Pray, have you not a daughter
> Called Katherina, fair and virtuous?

BAPTISTA
> I have a daughter, sir, called Katherina.

GREMIO
45 > *(to* PETRUCHIO*)* You are too blunt. Go to it orderly.

PETRUCHIO
> You wrong me, Signior Gremio. Give me leave.—
> I am a gentleman of Verona, sir,
> That hearing of her beauty and her wit,
> Her affability and bashful modesty,
50 > Her wondrous qualities and mild behavior,
> Am bold to show myself a forward guest
> Within your house, to make mine eye the witness
> Of that report which I so oft have heard.
> And, for an entrance to my entertainment,
55 > I do present you with a man of mine,
> *(presenting* HORTENSIO, *disguised as* LITIO*)*
> Cunning in music and the mathematics,
> To instruct her fully in those sciences,
> Whereof I know she is not ignorant.
> Accept of him, or else you do me wrong.
60 > His name is Litio, born in Mantua.

GREMIO *enters with* LUCENTIO, *dressed as a poor man;* PETRUCHIO *enters with* HORTENSIO, *disguised as a musician;* TRANIO, *disguised as* LUCENTIO, *enters with* BIONDELLO, *who is carrying a lute and books.*

GREMIO

Good morning, neighbor Baptista.

BAPTISTA

Good morning, neighbor Gremio. Greetings, gentlemen.

PETRUCHIO

And to you, good sir. Tell me, don't you have a virtuous and lovely daughter named Katherina?

BAPTISTA

I have a daughter named Katherina, sir.

GREMIO

(to PETRUCHIO*)* You are too blunt. You're supposed to work up to it.

PETRUCHIO

Please, Signior Gremio. Allow me to continue.—I am a gentleman of Verona, sir, who, hearing of your daughter's beauty and wit, her friendly disposition and bashful modesty, her uncommon virtues and her mild behavior, have taken the liberty of presenting myself as a guest at your house in the hope of seeing for myself if what I've heard is true. And, as the price of admission for being received by you, I here present you with a servant of mine. (*he presents* HORTENSIO, *disguised as* LITIO). He is expert in the fields of music and mathematics. I thought he might instruct her in those branches of knowledge—of which she is, I gather, no beginner. Be good enough to accept this gift—I'll be offended if you don't. His name is Litio, and he comes from Mantua.

BAPTISTA
> You're welcome, sir, and he for your good sake.
> But for my daughter Katherine, this I know,
> She is not for your turn, the more my grief.

PETRUCHIO
> I see you do not mean to part with her,
> 65   Or else you like not of my company.

BAPTISTA
> Mistake me not. I speak but as I find.
> Whence are you, sir? What may I call your name?

PETRUCHIO
> Petruchio is my name, Antonio's son,
> A man well known throughout all Italy.

BAPTISTA
> 70   I know him well. You are welcome for his sake.

GREMIO
> Saving your tale, Petruchio, I pray
> Let us that are poor petitioners speak too.
> *Bacare,* you are marvelous forward.

PETRUCHIO
> Oh, pardon me, Signior Gremio, I would fain be doing.

GREMIO
> 75   I doubt it not, sir, but you will curse your wooing.—
> Neighbor, this is a gift very grateful, I am sure of it. To
> express the like kindness, myself, that have been more
> kindly beholding to you than any, freely give unto you this
> young scholar *(presenting* LUCENTIO, *disguised as* CAMBIO*)*
> 80   that hath been long studying at Rheims, as cunning in
> Greek, Latin, and other languages as the other in music and
> mathematics. His name is Cambio. Pray accept his service.

BAPTISTA

You and he are both welcome, sir. As for my daughter Katherine, this much I know: she's not for you—more's the pity.

PETRUCHIO

I see you don't intend to part with her—or perhaps you don't like my company.

BAPTISTA

Don't misunderstand me, sir. I'm just stating the facts as I see them. Where are you from? What's your name?

PETRUCHIO

My name is Petruchio, son of Antonio, a man well known throughout Italy.

BAPTISTA

I know him well. You are welcome for his sake.

GREMIO

With all due respect, Petruchio, give someone else a chance to speak. You're *so* aggressive!

PETRUCHIO

Forgive me, Signior Gremio, but I'm anxious to get things moving.

GREMIO

No doubt, but you may be going about it the wrong way—Neighbor, this gift is very gracious, I'm sure. I myself, who am more indebted to you than anyone, have brought you this young scholar *(presenting* LUCENTIO, *disguised as* CAMBIO) who has long studied at Rheims. He is as expert in Greek, Latin, and other languages as that other man is in music and mathematics. His name is Cambio. Please accept his services.

Rheims was the site of a renowned university in France.

BAPTISTA
A thousand thanks, Signior Gremio. Welcome, good
Cambio. *(to* TRANIO *as* LUCENTIO*)* But, gentle sir, methinks
85   you walk like a stranger. May I be so bold to know the cause
of your coming?

TRANIO
(as LUCENTIO*)* Pardon me, sir, the boldness is mine own,
That being a stranger in this city here
Do make myself a suitor to your daughter,
90   Unto Bianca, fair and virtuous.
Nor is your firm resolve unknown to me,
In the preferment of the eldest sister.
This liberty is all that I request,
That, upon knowledge of my parentage,
95   I may have welcome 'mongst the rest that woo
And free access and favor as the rest.
And toward the education of your daughters,
I here bestow a simple instrument
And this small packet of Greek and Latin books.

BIONDELLO *brings the gifts forward*

100   If you accept them, then their worth is great.

BAPTISTA
Lucentio is your name. Of whence, I pray?

TRANIO
(as LUCENTIO*)* Of Pisa, sir, son to Vincentio.

BAPTISTA
A mighty man of Pisa. By report
I know him well. You are very welcome, sir.
105   *(to* HORTENSIO *as* LITIO*)* Take you the lute,
(to LUCENTIO *as* CAMBIO*)* and you the set of books.
You shall go see your pupils presently.
Holla, within!

Enter a Servant

BAPTISTA

Many thanks, Signior Gremio. Welcome, good Cambio. *(to* TRANIO *as* LUCENTIO*)* As for you, sir, you would appear to be a stranger. May I be so bold as to ask your reason for coming?

TRANIO

(as LUCENTIO*)* Pardon me, sir, the boldness is all mine in seeking to court your fair and virtuous daughter, Bianca. I am indeed a stranger in this city. I'm aware of your firm decision regarding her older sister. I only ask that when you know who my parents are, I may be made as welcome as her other suitors and given the same freedom and favor. My contribution toward the education of your daughters is a lute and this small package of Greek and Latin books. *(*BIONDELLO *brings the gifts forward)* You would add to their value by accepting them.

BAPTISTA

Your name is Lucentio, you say. Of what city, may I ask?

TRANIO

(as LUCENTIO*)* Of Pisa, sir, son of Vincentio.

BAPTISTA

A man of great influence. I know him well by reputation. You are very welcome here, sir. *(to* HORTENSIO *as* LITIO*)* You take the lute *(to* LUCENTIO *as* CAMBIO*)*, and you, the set of books. I'll send you to your pupils right away. You there in the house!

A servant enters.

Sirrah, lead these gentlemen
To my daughters, and tell them both
110   These are their tutors. Bid them use them well.

Exit Servant with LUCENTIO *and* HORTENSIO,
BIONDELLO *following*

We will go walk a little in the orchard,
And then to dinner. You are passing welcome,
And so I pray you all to think yourselves.

PETRUCHIO
Signior Baptista, my business asketh haste,
115   And every day I cannot come to woo.
You knew my father well, and in him me,
Left solely heir to all his lands and goods,
Which I have bettered rather than decreased.
Then tell me, if I get your daughter's love,
120   What dowry shall I have with her to wife?

BAPTISTA
After my death, the one half of my lands,
And, in possession, twenty thousand crowns.

PETRUCHIO
And, for that dowry, I'll assure her of
Her widowhood, be it that she survive me,
125   In all my lands and leases whatsoever.
Let specialties be therefore drawn between us,
That covenants may be kept on either hand.

BAPTISTA
Ay, when the special thing is well obtained,
That is, her love, for that is all in all.

PETRUCHIO
130   Why, that is nothing. For I tell you, father,
I am as peremptory as she proud-minded;
And where two raging fires meet together,
They do consume the thing that feeds their fury.

Boy, take these gentlemen to my daughters, and tell them both they are to be their teachers and to be courteous to them.

The servant exits with LUCENTIO *and* HORTENSIO, *followed by* BIONDELLO.

Let's take a little walk in the orchard before dinner. You are all most welcome here; please make yourselves at home.

PETRUCHIO

Signior Baptista, I'm actually in a bit of a hurry. I can't make this wooing into a daily thing. You knew my father well; therefore, you know me, the sole heir to all his property and possessions, which I have added to rather than depleted. So, tell me, assuming I win your daughter's love, what dowry would she bring to the marriage?

BAPTISTA

Twenty thousand crowns now, and half my lands after my death.

PETRUCHIO

Fair enough. And on my side, I'll guarantee that if I die before she does, she shall inherit all my land and the rent from any property I own. Let's have explicit contracts drawn up to ensure that both sides keep their promises.

BAPTISTA

Certainly, as soon as you've gotten the most important thing—her love. That counts for everything.

PETRUCHIO

Oh, that's nothing, believe me, sir. I'm as commanding as she is proud, and when two raging fires meet, they end up consuming the very thing that kindled them.

Though little fire grows great with little wind,
135   Yet extreme gusts will blow out fire and all.
So I to her and so she yields to me,
For I am rough and woo not like a babe.

BAPTISTA
Well mayst thou woo, and happy be thy speed.
But be thou armed for some unhappy words.

PETRUCHIO
140   Ay, to the proof, as mountains are for winds,
That shakes not, though they blow perpetually.

Enter HORTENSIO *as* LITIO, *with his head broke*

BAPTISTA
How now, my friend, why dost thou look so pale?

HORTENSIO
(as LITIO*)* For fear, I promise you, if I look pale.

BAPTISTA
What, will my daughter prove a good musician?

HORTENSIO
145   I think she'll sooner prove a soldier.
Iron may hold with her, but never lutes.

BAPTISTA
Why, then thou canst not break her to the lute?

HORTENSIO
Why, no, for she hath broke the lute to me.
I did but tell her she mistook her frets,
150   And bowed her hand to teach her fingering,
When, with a most impatient devilish spirit,
"'Frets' call you these?" quoth she. "I'll fume with them!"
And with that word she struck me on the head,
And through the instrument my pate made way,

Blow on a fire and all you do is fan the flames. But a great gust of wind will blow the fire out completely. I'm that great gust to her fire. I'm rough, and I don't woo like a little boy.

BAPTISTA

Well, good luck! I hope you're successful. But prepare yourself for some unpleasantness.

PETRUCHIO

I'll be completely prepared. Mountains don't tremble, however much the wind may blow!

Enter HORTENSIO *as* LITIO, *with his head cut and bleeding.*

BAPTISTA

Gracious! Why so pale, my friend?

HORTENSIO

(as LITIO*)* I would have to say from fear.

BAPTISTA

Will my daughter be a good musician, do you think?

HORTENSIO

I think she'll be a better soldier. She may be good with firearms. Never lutes.

BAPTISTA

You don't think you can teach her?

HORTENSIO

No, but she's taught me a thing or two! All I said was that she was using the wrong frets and tried to adjust her fingering. And she jumps up and says, "Frets? I'll give you frets!" With that, she clobbers me with the lute so that my head goes right through,

155   And there I stood amazèd for a while
        As on a pillory, looking through the lute,
        While she did call me "rascal fiddler"
        And "twangling Jack"; with twenty such vile terms,
        As had she studied to misuse me so.

PETRUCHIO
160   Now, by the world, it is a lusty wench.
        I love her ten times more than e'er I did.
        Oh, how I long to have some chat with her!

BAPTISTA
        (to HORTENSIO as LITIO)
        Well, go with me and be not so discomfited.
        Proceed in practice with my younger daughter.
165   She's apt to learn and thankful for good turns.
        Signior Petruchio, will you go with us,
        Or shall I send my daughter Kate to you?

PETRUCHIO
        I pray you do.

                              Exeunt all but PETRUCHIO
                    I'll attend her here
        And woo her with some spirit when she comes.
170   Say that she rail; why then I'll tell her plain
        She sings as sweetly as a nightingale.
        Say that she frown; I'll say she looks as clear
        As morning roses newly washed with dew.
        Say she be mute and will not speak a word;
175   Then I'll commend her volubility,
        And say she uttereth piercing eloquence.
        If she do bid me pack, I'll give her thanks,
        As though she bid me stay by her a week.
        If she deny to wed, I'll crave the day
180   When I shall ask the banns and when be marrièd.
        But here she comes—and now, Petruchio, speak.

and there I am, dazed, strings around my neck, looking through the sound hole like I was in the stocks, while she calls me "worthless fiddler," "twanging twerp," and twenty more hateful names, as though she'd prepared for me by composing a long list of insults to use on my behalf.

PETRUCHIO

I like this girl! She has real character! Now I want her more than ever. I can't wait to meet her!

BAPTISTA

(to HORTENSIO, *disguised as* LITIO*)* All right, come with me. Don't be discouraged. Continue your lessons with my younger daughter. She's quick to learn and responsive. Signior Petruchio, will you come with us, or shall I send my daughter Kate to you?

PETRUCHIO

Please do.

Everyone but PETRUCHIO *exits.*

I'll wait for her here and when she comes I'll take a novel approach with her. If she rants, I'll tell her that she sings as sweetly as a nightingale. If she glares, I'll say her brow is as clear as roses newly washed with morning dew. If she is silent and won't speak at all, I'll praise her chattiness and say she speaks with piercing eloquence. If she orders me to go, I'll thank her warmly as if she'd just offered to put me up for a week. If she refuses my proposal, I'll tell her how much I'm looking forward to the announcement and the wedding. But here she comes. Here goes!

Enter KATHERINE

Good morrow, Kate—for that's your name, I hear.

KATHERINE
Well have you heard, but something hard of hearing.
They call me Katherine that do talk of me.

PETRUCHIO
185 You lie, in faith, for you are called plain Kate,
And bonny Kate, and sometimes Kate the curst,
But Kate, the prettiest Kate in Christendom,
Kate of Kate Hall, my super-dainty Kate—
For dainties are all Kates—and therefore, Kate,
190 Take this of me, Kate of my consolation:
Hearing thy mildness praised in every town,
Thy virtues spoke of, and thy beauty sounded—
Yet not so deeply as to thee belongs—
Myself am moved to woo thee for my wife.

KATHERINE
195 "Moved," in good time. Let him that moved you hither
Remove you hence. I knew you at the first
You were a moveable.

PETRUCHIO
                    Why, what's a moveable?

KATHERINE
A joint stool.

PETRUCHIO
                    Thou hast hit it. Come, sit on me.

KATHERINE
Asses are made to bear, and so are you.

PETRUCHIO
200 Women are made to bear, and so are you.

KATHERINE *enters.*

Good morning, Kate, for I hear that's what you're called.

KATHERINE

Is that what you've heard? Then you'd better get your ears checked. I am called Katherine by those who have any business using my name.

PETRUCHIO

Liar. In fact, you're called Kate, plain Kate—and pretty Kate, and sometimes Kate the shrew. But it's definitely Kate—the prettiest Kate in the world, Katie, Kitty, Kat-woman, the Kate-ster—and so, Kate, here's my pitch: that having heard your charming disposition praised—not to mention your beauty and your virtues, though none of them as richly as you deserve—I find myself driven to propose. I want you for my wife.

KATHERINE

"Driven?" Really? Well, let whoever drove you here drive you back again. I had you figured for a piece of furniture.

PETRUCHIO

What do you mean by "furniture"?

KATHERINE

A nice stool.

PETRUCHIO

You're right, actually. Come sit on me.

KATHERINE

Asses are made for bearing, and so are you.

PETRUCHIO

A double pun—"to bear," here, means first "to bear weight" and second "to give birth to children."

Women are made for bearing, and so are you.

KATHERINE
No such jade as you, if me you mean.

PETRUCHIO
Alas, good Kate, I will not burden thee,
For knowing thee to be but young and light—

KATHERINE
Too light for such a swain as you to catch,
205   And yet as heavy as my weight should be.

PETRUCHIO
"Should be"—should buzz!

KATHERINE
Well ta'en, and like a buzzard.

PETRUCHIO
O slow-winged turtle, shall a buzzard take thee?

KATHERINE
Ay, for a turtle, as he takes a buzzard.

PETRUCHIO
Come, come, you wasp. I' faith, you are too angry.

KATHERINE
210   If I be waspish, best beware my sting.

PETRUCHIO
My remedy is then to pluck it out.

KATHERINE
Ay, if the fool could find it where it lies.

PETRUCHIO
Who knows not where a wasp does wear his sting?
In his tail.

KATHERINE
215   In his tongue.

PETRUCHIO
Whose tongue?

KATHERINE
Yours, if you talk of tales. And so farewell.

KATHERINE

Not by the likes of you!

PETRUCHIO

In Shakespeare's day, "light" could mean "loose," as in "a loose woman."

Oh heavens, Kate, I wouldn't think of burdening you. I know how light and carefree you are.

KATHERINE

Too light for a lout like you to catch—though no lighter than I should be.

PETRUCHIO

Should be? Maybe you *should be* the subject of some buzz!

KATHERINE

Buzz off, buzzard.

Buzzard was another word for "fool" or "useless person" because a buzzard was a kind of hawk that was useless for falconry.

PETRUCHIO

The turtledove was a symbol of faithful love.

If I'm a buzzard, you're a turtledove.

KATHERINE

Only a buzzard would think so.

PETRUCHIO

Come, my little wasp—you're too angry.

KATHERINE

If I'm a wasp, look out for my stinger.

PETRUCHIO

All I have to do is remove it.

KATHERINE

True, if a fool such as yourself could find it.

PETRUCHIO

Everyone knows where a wasp wears its stinger. In its tail.

KATHERINE

No, in its tongue.

PETRUCHIO

Whose tongue?

KATHERINE

Yours, if we're talking about tales. I'm leaving.

"Tales" here means "lies," as in "telling tales," and is a pun on "tail," which, when Petruchio first mentions it, means "butt." Their punning involves a lot of sexual innuendo.

PETRUCHIO
> What, with my tongue in your tail? Nay, come again,
> Good Kate. I am a gentleman.

KATHERINE
>   That I'll try.

She strikes him

PETRUCHIO
> I swear I'll cuff you if you strike again.

KATHERINE
220
> So may you lose your arms.
> If you strike me, you are no gentleman;
> And if no gentleman, why then no arms.

PETRUCHIO
> A herald, Kate? Oh, put me in thy books!

KATHERINE
> What is your crest? A coxcomb?

PETRUCHIO
225
> A combless cock, so Kate will be my hen.

KATHERINE
> No cock of mine. You crow too like a craven.

PETRUCHIO
> Nay, come, Kate, come. You must not look so sour.

KATHERINE
> It is my fashion, when I see a crab.

PETRUCHIO
> Why, here's no crab, and therefore look not sour.

KATHERINE
230
> There is, there is.

PETRUCHIO

You're leaving with my tongue in your tail? No, come back, Kate. I'm too much of a gentleman.

KATHERINE

A gentleman? We'll see about that!

She strikes him.

PETRUCHIO

I swear I'll smack you if you hit me again.

KATHERINE

A noble family, like that of a "gentleman," would have a "coat of arms."

Not if you want to keep your arms! If you hit me, that proves you're not a gentleman. And if you're not a gentleman, you don't have any arms.

PETRUCHIO

A herald's books officially registered gentlemen.

Are you a herald, Kate? Put me in your books!

KATHERINE

A crest is a symbol on a nobleman's family coat of arms.

What is your crest? A coxcomb?

A coxcomb was a dunce cap such as worn by fools and jesters.

PETRUCHIO

Cock = rooster. The comb was the symbol of a rooster's masculinity, so Petruchio is willing to be "unmanned" for her.

I'll give up my comb, if you'll be my hen.

KATHERINE

Your cock is not for me. It has no fighting spirit.

PETRUCHIO

Oh, come on now, Kate. Don't look so sour.

KATHERINE

That's my way, when I see a crab-apple.

PETRUCHIO

There's no crab-apple here, so don't look sour.

KATHERINE

There is a crab-apple here.

PETRUCHIO
Then show it me.

KATHERINE
Had I a glass, I would.

PETRUCHIO
What, you mean my face?

KATHERINE
Well aimed of such a young one.

PETRUCHIO
235   Now, by Saint George, I am too young for you.

KATHERINE
Yet you are withered.

PETRUCHIO
                    'Tis with cares.

KATHERINE
                                        I care not.

PETRUCHIO
Nay, hear you, Kate: in sooth you 'scape not so.

KATHERINE
I chafe you, if I tarry. Let me go.

PETRUCHIO
No, not a whit. I find you passing gentle.
240   'Twas told me you were rough and coy and sullen,
And now I find report a very liar.
For thou are pleasant, gamesome, passing courteous,
But slow in speech, yet sweet as springtime flowers.
Thou canst not frown, thou canst not look askance,
245   Nor bite the lip as angry wenches will,
Nor hast thou pleasure to be cross in talk.
But thou with mildness entertain'st thy wooers,
With gentle conference, soft and affable.
Why does the world report that Kate doth limp?

PETRUCHIO

Show me.

KATHERINE

I would, if I had a mirror.

PETRUCHIO

What, you mean my face looks like a crab-apple?

KATHERINE

What a clever child he is!

PETRUCHIO

You know, you're right. I probably am too young for you.

KATHERINE

Maybe, but you're wrinkled all the same.

PETRUCHIO

Oh, that's with worry.

KATHERINE

Well, that doesn't worry me.

PETRUCHIO

Listen, Kate! You won't get away like that.

KATHERINE

Let me go. I'll make you angry if I stay.

PETRUCHIO

No, not a bit. I find you quite gentle. I was told that you were violent, proud, and sullen. But now I see that people have been lying about you, for you are funny, playful, and beautifully behaved, not sharp-tongued, but as sweet as flowers in springtime. You haven't got it in you to frown or look displeased or bite your lip as angry women do. You don't take pleasure in bitter conversation. No, you entertain your suitors with mild and gentle conversation, quiet and pleasant. Why does the world report that Kate is lame?

250   O slanderous world! Kate like the hazel-twig
       Is straight and slender and as brown in hue
       As hazel nuts, and sweeter than the kernels.
       Oh, let me see thee walk! Thou dost not halt.

KATHERINE
       Go, fool, and whom thou keep'st command.

PETRUCHIO
255   Did ever Dian so become a grove
       As Kate this chamber with her princely gait?
       Oh, be thou Dian, and let her be Kate,
       And then let Kate be chaste and Dian sportful.

KATHERINE
       Where did you study all this goodly speech?

PETRUCHIO
260   It is extempore, from my mother wit.

KATHERINE
       A witty mother! Witless else her son.

PETRUCHIO
       Am I not wise?

KATHERINE
                          Yes, keep you warm.

PETRUCHIO
       Marry, so I mean, sweet Katherine, in thy bed.
       And therefore, setting all this chat aside,
265   Thus in plain terms: your father hath consented
       That you shall be my wife, your dowry 'greed on,
       And, will you, nill you, I will marry you.
       Now, Kate, I am a husband for your turn,
       For, by this light, whereby I see thy beauty,
270   Thy beauty that doth make me like thee well,
       Thou must be married to no man but me.
       For I am he am born to tame you, Kate,
       And bring you from a wild Kate to a Kate
       Conformable as other household Kates.

The world's a liar. Kate is as straight and slender as a hazel-twig, her hair as brown as hazelnut shells, and she herself sweeter than the kernels. Take a few steps—I want to see you walk. You don't limp at all!

KATHERINE

Get out of here, fool, and give orders to your servants, not me.

PETRUCHIO

Did Diana ever beautify a grove as much as Kate beautifies this room with her queenly movements? You be Diana, and let Diana be Kate. Then let Kate be the chaste one, while Diana plays with me.

KATHERINE

Where do you memorize all this smart talk?

PETRUCHIO

Mother wit = natural intelligence. I make it up as I go. It's born of my mother wit.

KATHERINE

A witty mother! Too bad about the son!

PETRUCHIO

Am I not wise?

KATHERINE

"Enough wit to keep yourself warm" was a proverbial expression for "stupid." Enough to keep yourself warm.

PETRUCHIO

Yes, I intend to keep myself warm, sweet Katherine— in your bed. So let's cut to the chase: your father has consented for you to become my wife. Your dowry is agreed upon, and whether you like it or not, I will marry you. I tell you, I'm the man for you, Kate. I swear by this light, which shows me your beauty—the beauty that makes me love you—that you must be married to no man but me. I'm the man who was born to tame you and change you from a wildcat Kate into a Kate as gentle and domestic as other household Kates.

Enter BAPTISTA, GREMIO, *and* TRANIO

275   Here comes your father. Never make denial.
        I must and will have Katherine to my wife.

BAPTISTA
        Now, Signior Petruchio, how speed you with my daughter?

PETRUCHIO
        How but well, sir? How but well?
        It were impossible I should speed amiss.

BAPTISTA
280   Why, how now, daughter Katherine? In your dumps?

KATHERINE
        Call you me daughter? Now, I promise you
        You have showed a tender fatherly regard
        To wish me wed to one half lunatic,
        A mad-cup ruffian and a swearing Jack,
285   That thinks with oaths to face the matter out.

PETRUCHIO
        Father, 'tis thus: yourself and all the world
        That talked of her have talked amiss of her.
        If she be curst, it is for policy,
        For she's not froward, but modest as the dove.
290   She is not hot, but temperate as the morn.
        For patience she will prove a second Grissel,
        And Roman Lucrece for her chastity.
        And to conclude, we have 'greed so well together,
        That upon Sunday is the wedding day.

KATHERINE
295   I'll see thee hanged on Sunday first.

GREMIO
        Hark, Petruchio: she says she'll see thee hanged first.

BAPTISTA, GREMIO, *and* TRANIO *enter.*

Here comes your father. Don't even think about refusing. I must and will have Katherine for my wife.

BAPTISTA

Now, Signior Petruchio, how are you getting on with my daughter?

PETRUCHIO

Beautifully, sir, beautifully! It couldn't go any other way.

BAPTISTA

Now, daughter Katherine? Are you down in the dumps?

KATHERINE

You have the nerve to call me daughter? Is this a father's loving care—wanting to marry me off to a total madman, a worthless, irresponsible louse who thinks if he swears enough, he'll get his way?

PETRUCHIO

Sir, this is the truth: you and the rest—all the people who have ever talked about her—have all been wrong. If she seems fierce, it's for a reason. She's not obstinate but gentle as the dove, not high-strung but peaceful as the morning. She has the patience of a Griselda and the modesty of Rome's Lucrece. In short, we've gotten along so well that Sunday is our wedding day.

Griselda was a much put-upon wife in medieval song and story. Lucretia was the wife of a Roman senator, famous for her chastity.

KATHERINE

I'll see you hanged on Sunday first!

GREMIO

Listen to that Petruchio: she says she'll see you hanged first.

TRANIO
    Is this your speeding? Nay, then, good night our part.

PETRUCHIO
    Be patient, gentlemen. I choose her for myself.
    If she and I be pleased, what's that to you?
300   'Tis bargained 'twixt us twain, being alone,
    That she shall still be curst in company.
    I tell you, 'tis incredible to believe
    How much she loves me. O, the kindest Kate!
    She hung about my neck, and kiss on kiss
305   She vied so fast, protesting oath on oath,
    That in a twink she won me to her love.
    O, you are novices! 'Tis a world to see,
    How tame, when men and women are alone,
    A meacock wretch can make the curstest shrew.—
310   Give me thy hand, Kate. I will unto Venice
    To buy apparel 'gainst the wedding day.
    Provide the feast, father, and bid the guests.
    I will be sure my Katherine shall be fine.

BAPTISTA
    I know not what to say, but give me your hands.
315   God send you joy, Petruchio. 'Tis a match.

GREMIO *AND* TRANIO
    Amen, say we. We will be witnesses.

PETRUCHIO
    Father, and wife, and gentlemen, adieu.
    I will to Venice. Sunday comes apace.
    We will have rings, and things, and fine array,
320   And kiss me, Kate. We will be married o' Sunday.

                  Exeunt PETRUCHIO *and* KATHERINE *severally*

GREMIO
    Was ever match clapped up so suddenly?

BAPTISTA
    Faith, gentlemen, now I play a merchant's part,
    And venture madly on a desperate mart.

TRANIO

Is this your idea of success? So much for our plan.

PETRUCHIO

Relax, gentlemen. I've made my choice. If she and I are happy, what's it to you? When we were alone, we agreed that in public she would go on being unpleasant. I tell you, though, it's incredible how much she loves me. Darling Kate! She hung about my neck, smothering me with kisses, making vow after vow. In this way, she won my heart lickety-split! You men are rank beginners! It's amazing how even a timid wretch can tame the most dreadful shrew, if the two are left alone together. Give me your hand, Kate. I'm off to Venice to buy outfits for the wedding. Plan the feast, sir, and invite the guests. I want my Katherine decked out in the finest clothes.

BAPTISTA

I don't know what to say. Well, give me your hands. God give you joy, Petruchio. Call it a match!

GREMIO *AND* TRANIO

Amen to that! We'll be your witnesses.

PETRUCHIO

Father, wife, friends—farewell! I'm off to Venice. Sunday is just around the corner. We will have rings and things and fancy dress! So kiss me, Kate. We're to be married on Sunday.

PETRUCHIO *and* KATHERINE *exit in different directions.*

GREMIO

Was there ever a match put together so quickly?

BAPTISTA

Truly, gentlemen, this is a chancy piece of business. I've made a risky investment.

TRANIO
(as LUCENTIO) 'Twas a commodity lay fretting by you.
325   'Twill bring you gain or perish on the seas.

BAPTISTA
The gain I seek is quiet in the match.

GREMIO
No doubt but he hath got a quiet catch.
But now, Baptista, to your younger daughter.
Now is the day we long have lookèd for.
330   I am your neighbor, and was suitor first.

TRANIO
(as LUCENTIO) And I am one that love Bianca more
Than words can witness or your thoughts can guess.

GREMIO
Youngling, thou canst not love so dear as I.

TRANIO
(as LUCENTIO)
Graybeard, thy love doth freeze.

GREMIO
                                    But thine doth fry.
335   Skipper, stand back. 'Tis age that nourisheth.

TRANIO
(as LUCENTIO) But youth in ladies' eyes that flourisheth.

BAPTISTA
Content you, gentlemen. I will compound this strife.
'Tis deeds must win the prize, and he of both
That can assure my daughter greatest dower
340   Shall have my Bianca's love.
Say, Signior Gremio, what can you assure her?

TRANIO

(*speaking as* LUCENTIO) Yes, but the item was just gathering dust. This way, you'll either make a profit by it or lose it on the high seas.

BAPTISTA

The only profit I seek is a peaceful match.

GREMIO

There's no doubt that Petruchio's got quite a catch. Now, Baptista, let's turn to your younger daughter. We've been waiting a long time for this day. I'm your neighbor and came courting first.

TRANIO

(*speaking as* LUCENTIO) And I am one who loves Bianca more than words can express, more than you can imagine.

GREMIO

Callow youth, you don't yet know how to love!

TRANIO

(*speaking as* LUCENTIO) Old man, your love is ice.

GREMIO

And you're all sizzle. Stand back, boy. Age is the thing that nourishes.

TRANIO

(*speaking as* LUCENTIO) Yes, but in the ladies' eyes, it's youth that flourishes.

BAPTISTA

"Deeds" is a pun; it means both actions (as opposed to words) and the legal documents for property and real estate.

Enough, gentlemen. I will settle this matter. Deeds will determine the winner here. Whichever of you can promise Bianca the greatest dower shall have my daughter's love. Tell me, Signior Gremio, what can you offer her?

GREMIO

First, as you know, my house within the city
Is richly furnishèd with plate and gold,
Basins and ewers to lave her dainty hands;
345   My hangings all of Tyrian tapestry,
In ivory coffers I have stuffed my crowns,
In cypress chests my arras counterpoints,
Costly apparel, tents, and canopies,
Fine linen, Turkey cushions bossed with pearl,
350   Valance of Venice gold in needlework,
Pewter and brass, and all things that belong
To house or housekeeping. Then, at my farm
I have a hundred milch-kine to the pail,
Six score fat oxen standing in my stalls,
355   And all things answerable to this portion.
Myself am struck in years, I must confess,
And if I die tomorrow this is hers,
If whilst I live she will be only mine.

TRANIO

(as LUCENTIO*)*

That "only" came well in. *(to* BAPTISTA*)* Sir, list to me:
360   I am my father's heir and only son.
If I may have your daughter to my wife,
I'll leave her houses three or four as good,
Within rich Pisa walls, as any one
Old Signior Gremio has in Padua,
365   Besides two thousand ducats by the year
Of fruitful land, all which shall be her jointure.—
What, have I pinched you, Signior Gremio?

GREMIO

Two thousand ducats by the year of land!
(aside) My land amounts not to so much in all.—
370   That she shall have, besides an argosy
That now is lying in Marcellus' road.
(to TRANIO*)* What, have I choked you with an argosy?

GREMIO

First of all, my house in the city, as you know, is filled with expensive furniture and household articles, china and gold, basins and pitchers for her to wash her dainty hands in. All my wall hangings are tapestries from Tyre. My ivory strongboxes are stuffed with gold, my wooden trunks filled with elegant rugs, expensive clothing, hangings and bed curtains, fine linens, Turkish cushions trimmed with pearls, Venetian draperies, pewter and brass, and everything else a household could possibly want. Then, at my farm I have a hundred milk cows, a hundred and twenty fat oxen in my stables, and all the equipment necessary to maintain them. I'm getting on in years, and if I died tomorrow, all this will belong to Bianca—if only while I live she'll belong solely to me.

TRANIO

(speaking as LUCENTIO*)* That "solely" is very much to the point. *(to* BAPTISTA*)* Sir, hear me out: I am my father's only son and, as such, his *sole* heir. If you give me your daughter's hand in marriage, she will end up with three or four houses in Pisa as good as any one that Gremio has in Padua—not to mention the two thousand ducats a year that my land earns me. All of which I'll leave her in my will. Did I see you flinch, Signior Gremio?

GREMIO

Two thousand ducats a year from his land! *(to himself)* All my land together isn't worth that much!—Aha! I forgot to mention the merchant ship that lies in Marseilles harbor. *(to* TRANIO*)* Sorry—have I caught you choking on a merchant ship?

TRANIO

    (as LUCENTIO*)* Gremio, 'tis known my father hath no less

    Than three great argosies, besides two galliasses,

375   And twelve tight galleys. These I will assure her,

    And twice as much whate'er thou offer'st next.

GREMIO

    Nay, I have offered all, I have no more,

    And she can have no more than all I have.

    (to BAPTISTA*)* If you like me, she shall have me and mine.

TRANIO

    (as LUCENTIO*)*

380   Why, then the maid is mine from all the world,

    By your firm promise. Gremio is outvied.

BAPTISTA

    I must confess your offer is the best,

    And, let your father make her the assurance,

    She is your own; else, you must pardon me.

385   If you should die before him, where's her dower?

TRANIO

    (as LUCENTIO*)* That's but a cavil: he is old, I young.

GREMIO

    And may not young men die as well as old?

BAPTISTA

    Well, gentlemen, I am thus resolved:

    On Sunday next, you know

390   My daughter Katherina is to be married.

    (to TRANIO *as* LUCENTIO*)*

    Now, on the Sunday following, shall Bianca

    Be bride to you, if you make this assurance.

    If not, to Signior Gremio.

    And so I take my leave, and thank you both.

TRANIO

> (speaking as LUCENTIO) Please, Gremio! Everyone knows that my father has no less than three, huge merchant ships and fourteen galleys—two large and twelve small. These also I promise to Bianca—and whatever your next offer is, I'll double it.

GREMIO

> I have nothing else to offer. That's everything I own. I can't offer her more than all I have. (to BAPTISTA) If you choose me, she shall have me and mine.

TRANIO

> (speaking as LUCENTIO) In that case I, of all the men in the world, have won the maid, by your explicit promise. Gremio is outbid.

BAPTISTA

> I must admit your offer is the best. And provided that your father will be your guarantor, she shall be yours. Otherwise—forgive me, but if you should die before him, what becomes of her dowry?

TRANIO

> (speaking as LUCENTIO) That's nothing! He is old, I'm young.

GREMIO

> Oh, and young men never die?

BAPTISTA

> Well, gentlemen, that's my decision. As you know, next Sunday my daughter Katherina is to be married. (to TRANIO as LUCENTIO) Therefore, the Sunday after, Bianca shall be married to you—if you obtain that guarantee. If not, she'll be married to Signior Gremio. And so I thank you both and bid you goodbye.

GREMIO
395   Adieu, good neighbor.

Exit BAPTISTA

        Now I fear thee not.
Sirrah young gamester, your father were a fool
To give thee all and in his waning age
Set foot under thy table. Tut, a toy!
An old Italian fox is not so kind, my boy.

Exit

TRANIO
400   A vengeance on your crafty withered hide!
Yet I have faced it with a card of ten.
'Tis in my head to do my master good.
I see no reason but supposed Lucentio
Must get a father, called "supposed Vincentio"—
405   And that's a wonder. Fathers commonly
Do get their children. But in this case of wooing,
A child shall get a sire, if I fail not of my cunning.

Exit

GREMIO

> Farewell, good neighbor.

> *BAPTISTA exits.*

> Now I'm not worried. You there, young sport! Your father would be a fool to give you all his wealth and spend his declining years as a guest in your house. It's absurd. An old Italian fox is never that generous, my boy.

> *He exits.*

TRANIO

> Sneaky, dried-up old coot! We'll see who gets the upper hand! I've already bluffed pretty well—and without even a face card. I have a mind to help my master. Clearly, the fake Lucentio will have to produce a father—call him "fake Vincentio"—and it will be a miracle. Usually fathers produce children, not the other way around. But in this case of wooing, a child shall father his own father—if my wits don't fail me.

> *He exits.*

ACT THREE
SCENE 1

Enter LUCENTIO *disguised as* CAMBIO, HORTENSIO *disguised as* LITIO, *and* BIANCA

LUCENTIO

(as CAMBIO*)* Fiddler, forbear. You grow too forward, sir.
Have you so soon forgot the entertainment
Her sister Katherina welcomed you withal?

HORTENSIO

(as LITIO*)* But, wrangling pedant, this is
5   The patroness of heavenly harmony.
Then give me leave to have prerogative,
And when in music we have spent an hour,
Your lecture shall have leisure for as much.

LUCENTIO

(as CAMBIO*)* Preposterous ass, that never read so far
10   To know the cause why music was ordained.
Was it not to refresh the mind of man
After his studies or his usual pain?
Then give me leave to read philosophy
And, while I pause, serve in your harmony.

HORTENSIO

15   *(as* LITIO*)* Sirrah, I will not bear these braves of thine.

BIANCA

Why, gentlemen, you do me double wrong
To strive for that which resteth in my choice.
I am no breeching scholar in the schools.
I'll not be tied to hours nor 'pointed times
20   But learn my lessons as I please myself.
And, to cut off all strife, here sit we down.

ACT THREE
SCENE 1

BIANCA *enters with* LUCENTIO *disguised as* CAMBIO, *and*
HORTENSIO *disguised as* LITIO

LUCENTIO

(*speaking as* CAMBIO) Restrain yourself, fiddler! You're too insistent. Have you forgotten how her sister Katherine thanked you for your lessons?

HORTENSIO

(*speaking as* LITIO) Quarrelsome teacher! This lady is the queen of heavenly harmony. Therefore allow me to claim her attention first, and after we have spent an hour on music you can have equal time for your lecture.

LUCENTIO

(*as* CAMBIO) Ridiculous ass! You're not even educated enough to know why music was created. Wasn't it to refresh the mind of man *after* his studies and daily toil? Therefore allow me to read philosophy with her, and then, when I am finished, indulge in your harmony.

HORTENSIO

(*as* LITIO) Sir, you go too far! I will not stand for it!

BIANCA

Gentlemen, it seems to me you're both out of line to be laying down the law about things that are really up to me. I am no schoolboy, and I won't be dictated to with hours and schedules. I'll have my lessons in the order and manner *I* prefer. So to cut short this argument, let's figure this out.

(to HORTENSIO*)*
Take you your instrument, play you the whiles.
His lecture will be done ere you have tuned.

HORTENSIO
(as LITIO*)* You'll leave his lecture when I am in tune?

LUCENTIO
25   *(aside)* That will be never. *(to* HORTENSIO*)* Tune your
instrument.

BIANCA
Where left we last?

LUCENTIO
Here, madam:
Hic ibat Simois, hic est Sigeia tellus,
30   *Hic steterat Priami regia celsa senis.*

BIANCA
Conster them.

LUCENTIO
Hic ibat, as I told you before, Simois, I am Lucentio, hic est,
son unto Vincentio of Pisa, Sigeia tellus, disguised thus to
get your love, Hic steterat, and that "Lucentio" that comes
35   a-wooing, Priami is my man Tranio, regia, bearing my port,
celsa senis, that we might beguile the old pantaloon.

HORTENSIO
(as LITIO*)* Madam, my instrument's in tune.

BIANCA
Let's hear. *(he plays)* O fie! The treble jars.

LUCENTIO
(as CAMBIO*)* Spit in the hole, man, and tune again.

(to HORTENSIO*)* You take your instrument and play awhile. He'll be finished with his lecture before you've even tuned it.

HORTENSIO

(as LITIO*)* You'll leave his lecture when I'm in tune?

LUCENTIO

(to himself) That will be never. *(to* HORTENSIO*)* Tune your instrument.

BIANCA

Where did we leave off?

LUCENTIO

Here, madam:

Hic ibat Simois, hic est Sigeia tellus,
Hic steterat Priami regia celsa senis.

> A line from Ovid.

BIANCA

Translate.

LUCENTIO

> Properly translated: "Here ran the Simois river, here is the Sigeian land, here stood the sky-high palace of old Priam."

Hic ibat, as I told you before, *Simois,* I am Lucentio, *hic est,* son of Vincentio of Pisa, *Sigeia tellus,* disguised as a teacher so as to win your love, *Hic steterat,* and the fellow who comes to court you calling himself "Lucentio," *Priami,* is my servant Tranio, *regia,* pretending to be me, *celsa senis,* so we can get the better of the foolish old man.

HORTENSIO

(as LITIO*)* Madam, my instrument's in tune.

BIANCA

Let's hear. *(he plays)* Oooh, no! The high note's off.

LUCENTIO

(as CAMBIO*)* Spit on the tuning-peg, man, and try again.

BIANCA

40   Now let me see if I can conster it. Hic ibat Simois, I know
        you not, hic est Sigeia tellus, I trust you not, Hic steterat
        Priami, take heed he hear us not, regia, presume not, celsa
        senis, despair not.

HORTENSIO

        (as LITIO*)* Madam, 'tis now in tune.

LUCENTIO

        (as CAMBIO*)*   All but the base.

HORTENSIO

45   *(as* LITIO*)*The base is right; 'tis the base knave that jars.
        (aside) How fiery and forward our pedant is!
        Now, for my life, the knave doth court my love.
        Pedascule, I'll watch you better yet.

BIANCA

        (to LUCENTIO*)* In time I may believe, yet I mistrust.

LUCENTIO

50   Mistrust it not, for sure Aeacides
        Was Ajax, called so from his grandfather.

BIANCA

        I must believe my master; else, I promise you,
        I should be arguing still upon that doubt.
        But let it rest.—Now, Litio, to you.
55   Good master, take it not unkindly, pray,
        That I have been thus pleasant with you both.

HORTENSIO

        (as LITIO, *to* LUCENTIO*)*
        You may go walk, and give me leave awhile.
        My lessons make no music in three parts.

BIANCA

Now let me see if I can translate it. *Hic ibat Simois,* I don't know you, *hic est Sigeia tellus,* I don't trust you, *Hic steterat Priami,* don't let him hear you, *regia,* don't take anything for granted, *celsa senis,* don't give up.

HORTENSIO

(as LITIO*)* Madam, now it really is in tune.

LUCENTIO

(as CAMBIO*)* All but the low note.

HORTENSIO

(as LITIO*)* The low note's fine; it's this low-minded dog that's out of tune! *(to himself)* How touchy and insistent this fellow is! I'm beginning to think he's wooing my darling. Little professor! I'll have to keep an eye on you.

BIANCA

(to LUCENTIO*)* In time I may come to believe you, but I'm wary.

LUCENTIO

There's no need to be, really, for— *(he breaks off, seeing that* HORTENSIO *is listening, and pretends to go back to the Latin lesson)* —"Aeacides" is just another name for Ajax. He gets it from his grandfather.

BIANCA

You're my teacher, so I must believe you. Otherwise, I would have to argue the point with you. But let it go.—Now, Litio, it's your turn. I hope, sir, that you're not angry that I've been equally attentive to you both!

HORTENSIO

(as LITIO*, to* LUCENTIO*)* You can take a break. Leave us alone, why don't you? I don't teach music for a threesome.

LUCENTIO

(as CAMBIO*)* Are you so formal, sir? Well, I must wait.
60   *(aside)* And watch withal, for, but I be deceived,
        Our fine musician groweth amorous.

HORTENSIO

(as LITIO*)* Madam, before you touch the instrument,
        To learn the order of my fingering
        I must begin with rudiments of art,
65   To teach you gamut in a briefer sort,
        More pleasant, pithy, and effectual
        Than hath been taught by any of my trade.
        And there it is in writing, fairly drawn.

BIANCA

        Why, I am past my gamut long ago.

HORTENSIO

70   Yet read the gamut of Hortensio.

BIANCA

        (reads)
        "*Gamut* I am, the ground of all accord:
        A re, to plead Hortensio's passion;
        B mi, Bianca, take him for thy lord,
        C fa ut, that loves with all affection;
75   *D sol re,* one clef, two notes have I;
        E la mi, show pity, or I die."
        Call you this "gamut"? Tut, I like it not.
        Old fashions please me best. I am not so nice
        To change true rules for old inventions.

        Enter a SERVANT

LUCENTIO

(*as* CAMBIO) Well, aren't we strict! Okay, I guess I'll have to wait. (*to himself*) And watch, too. For unless I'm very much mistaken, our fancy musician is turning romantic!

HORTENSIO

(*as* LITIO) Madam, before you take up the instrument or begin to learn the fingering, I must teach you certain fundamentals. To help you remember the scales, I've come up with a little trick—more fun and effective than those that any of my colleagues use. Here, I've written it out.

BIANCA

I think I know my scales by now!

HORTENSIO

(*speaking as* LITIO) Well, read Hortensio's scale anyway.

BIANCA

(*reading*)
"I am the scale, the basis of all harmony.
A re, Im here to argue for Hortensio's love;
B mi, Bianca, take him for your husband,
C fa ut, he loves you with all affection;
D sol re, I have one clef but only two notes;
E la mi, have pity on me, or I'll die."
You call this a scale? I don't like it. I don't go in for these new-fangled methods. I like doing things the old-fashioned way.

A SERVANT *enters.*

SERVANT
80   Mistress, your father prays you leave your books
       And help to dress your sister's chamber up.
       You know tomorrow is the wedding day.

BIANCA
       Farewell, sweet masters both. I must be gone.

LUCENTIO
       (*as* CAMBIO) Faith, mistress, then I have no cause to stay.

Exeunt BIANCA, *the* SERVANT, *and* LUCENTIO

HORTENSIO
85   But I have cause to pry into this pedant.
       Methinks he looks as though he were in love.
       Yet if thy thoughts, Bianca, be so humble
       To cast thy wand'ring eyes on every stale,
       Seize thee that list! If once I find thee ranging,
90   Hortensio will be quit with thee by changing.

Exit

SERVANT

> Mistress, your father requests that you leave your books and come help decorate your sister's room. You know tomorrow is her wedding day.

BIANCA

> Farewell to both of you, dear teachers. I have to go.

LUCENTIO

> *(as* CAMBIO*)* In that case, mistress, there's no reason for me to stay.

BIANCA, *the* SERVANT, *and* LUCENTIO *exit.*

HORTENSIO

> But there's reason for me to look more closely at this schoolmaster. He acts like a man in love. But if Bianca is so vulgar as to stoop for any man she sees, the hell with her. Whoever wants her can have her. The first time I catch her straying, it's over. End of story.

He exits.

ACT 3, SCENE 2

Enter BAPTISTA, GREMIO, TRANIO *as* LUCENTIO, KATHERINE, BIANCA, LUCENTIO, *and others, attendants*

BAPTISTA
    (to TRANIO*)* Signior Lucentio, this is the 'pointed day
    That Katherine and Petruchio should be married,
    And yet we hear not of our son-in-law.
    What will be said? What mockery will it be,
5   To want the bridegroom when the priest attends
    To speak the ceremonial rites of marriage?
    What says Lucentio to this shame of ours?

KATHERINE
    No shame but mine. I must, forsooth, be forced
    To give my hand, opposed against my heart,
10   Unto a mad-brain rudesby, full of spleen,
    Who wooed in haste and means to wed at leisure.
    I told you, I, he was a frantic fool,
    Hiding his bitter jests in blunt behavior,
    And, to be noted for a merry man,
15   He'll woo a thousand, 'point the day of marriage,
    Make friends, invite, and proclaim the banns,
    Yet never means to wed where he hath wooed.
    Now must the world point at poor Katherine
    And say, "Lo, there is mad Petruchio's wife,
20   If it would please him come and marry her!"

TRANIO
    (as LUCENTIO*)* Patience, good Katherine, and Baptista too.
    Upon my life, Petruchio means but well,
    Whatever fortune stays him from his word:
    Though he be blunt, I know him passing wise;
25   Though he be merry, yet withal he's honest.

ACT 3, SCENE 2

BAPTISTA *and* GREMIO *enter, followed by* TRANIO *disguised as* LUCENTIO, KATHERINE, BIANCA, LUCENTIO, *and servants.*

BAPTISTA

(to TRANIO *as* LUCENTIO*)* Signior Lucentio, this is the day appointed for Katherine and Petruchio's wedding, but there's no sign of the groom. What will people say? To have the priest right here, ready to perform the marriage ceremony, and be missing a bridegroom! What do you think about our humiliation, Lucentio?

KATHERINE

The humiliation is all mine. You forced me to accept this man against my will, this fancy con artist who was in such a hurry to get engaged. He has no intention of marrying me. I knew it—I told you. The whole thing was a joke. He pretends to be this simple, backward guy, but it's all a gag to amuse his witty friends. He goes around proposing to women—they set a date, he gets introduced around, they send out the invitations and make a public announcement, but he has no intention of going through with it. So now everyone will point at me and say, "Look, there goes the wife of that comedian Petruchio—if he could be bothered to marry the pathetic thing!"

TRANIO

(speaking as LUCENTIO*)* No, no, I assure you, Katherine—and you, too, Baptista—Petruchio means well, whatever circumstance prevents him from keeping his word. He's rough-edged, but he's a good man, and though he likes a joke, he's not a liar.

KATHERINE
Would Katherine had never seen him, though!

Exit weeping, followed by BIANCA *and others*

BAPTISTA
Go, girl. I cannot blame thee now to weep,
For such an injury would vex a very saint,
Much more a shrew of thy impatient humor.

Enter BIONDELLO

BIONDELLO
30   Master, master! News, old news, and such news as you
never heard of!

BAPTISTA
Is it new and old too? How may that be?

BIONDELLO
Why, is it not news to hear of Petruchio's coming?

BAPTISTA
Is he come?

BIONDELLO
35   Why, no, sir.

BAPTISTA
What then?

BIONDELLO
He is coming.

BAPTISTA
When will he be here?

BIONDELLO
When he stands where I am and sees you there.

TRANIO
40   *(as* LUCENTIO*)* But say, what to thine old news?

KATHERINE

> Maybe, but I wish I'd never laid eyes on him.

She exits weeping, followed by BIANCA *and others.*

BAPTISTA

> Go, daughter. I cannot blame you now for weeping.
> An insult like this would try the patience of a saint, let
> alone a hot-tempered shrew like you!

BIONDELLO *enters.*

BIONDELLO

> Master, master! I have news—old news such as you
> never heard before!

BAPTISTA

> You say you have news that's old? How can that be?

BIONDELLO

> Well, is it not news that Petruchio's coming?

BAPTISTA

> Is he here?

BIONDELLO

> Why, no, sir.

BAPTISTA

> What then?

BIONDELLO

> He is coming.

BAPTISTA

> When will he be here?

BIONDELLO

> When he stands where I am and sees you there.

TRANIO

> *(as* LUCENTIO*)* So what's the *old* news?

BIONDELLO

Why, Petruchio is coming in a new hat and an old jerkin, a
pair of old breeches thrice turned, a pair of boots that have
been candle cases, one buckled, another laced; an old rusty
sword ta'en out of the town armory, with a broken hilt and
45   chapeless; with two broken points; his horse hipped, with
an old mothy saddle and stirrups of no kindred, besides
possessed with the glanders and like to mose in the chine,
troubled with the lampass, infected with the fashions, full
of wingdalls, sped with spavins, rayed with yellows, past
50   cure of the fives, stark spoiled with the staggers, begnawn
with the bots, swayed in the back and shoulder-shotten,
near-legged before and with a half-checked bit and a
headstall of sheeps leather, which, being restrained to keep
him from stumbling, hath been often burst, and now
55   repaired with knots, one girth six times pieced, and a
woman's crupper of velour, which hath two letters for her
name fairly set down in studs, and here and there pieced
with packthread.

BAPTISTA

Who comes with him?

BIONDELLO

60   O, sir, his lackey, for all the world caparisoned like the
horse; with a linen stock on one leg and a kersey boot-hose
on the other, gartered with a red and blue list; an old hat and
the humor of forty fancies pricked in 't for a feather. A
monster, a very monster in apparel, and not like a Christian
65   footboy or a gentleman's lackey.

TRANIO

(*as* **LUCENTIO**)

'Tis some odd humor pricks him to this fashion,
Yet oftentimes he goes but mean-appareled.

BAPTISTA

I am glad he's come, howsoe'er he comes.

BIONDELLO

> Well, Petruchio is coming in a new hat and an old vest, a pair of old pants turned inside out, unmatched boots that have been used as spittoons, one buckled, the other laced; a rusty old sword from the town armory with a broken hilt and no scabbard. He's got on worn-out garters and is riding a swayback old horse with a moth-eaten saddle, stirrups from two different sets, a bad hip, swollen glands, lockjaw, leg ulcers, bedsores, arthritis, jaundice, a hernia, hives, worms, cancer, a mossy overbite, and post-nasal drip. He's knock-kneed too. His bit's lopsided and his cardboard bridle, which breaks when you pull on it, is taped in a few places. The saddle strap is made out of patchwork, and the strap that goes under his tail to keep the saddle in place is velvet, with the initials of some woman written in studs.

BAPTISTA

> Who comes with him?

BIONDELLO

> Just his servant, sir—pretty much got up like the horse, with a linen stocking on one leg and a big woolen booty on the other, a pair of red and blue garters, and an old hat with something no one's ever seen before where the feather should be. He's dressed like a freak, a total freak, and not at all like a proper footman or a gentleman's valet.

TRANIO

> (*as* LUCENTIO) He must be in a strange mood to go in for this fashion—though from time to time he *has* been known to dress down.

BAPTISTA

> I am glad he's coming, however he's dressed.

BIONDELLO
> Why, sir, he comes not.

BAPTISTA
70 > Didst thou not say he comes?

BIONDELLO
> Who? That Petruchio came?

BAPTISTA
> Ay, that Petruchio came.

BIONDELLO
> No, sir, I say his horse comes, with him on his back.

BAPTISTA
> Why, that's all one.

BIONDELLO
75 > Nay, by Saint Jamy,
> I hold you a penny,
> A horse and a man
> Is more than one
> And yet not many.

Enter PETRUCHIO *and* GRUMIO

PETRUCHIO
80 > Come, where be these gallants? Who's at home?

BAPTISTA
> You are welcome, sir.

PETRUCHIO
> And yet I come not well.

BAPTISTA
> And yet you halt not.

TRANIO
> *(as* LUCENTIO*)* Not so well appareled as I wish you were.

BIONDELLO

Why, sir, he's not coming.

BAPTISTA

Didn't you just say he was?

BIONDELLO

Who? Petruchio?

BAPTISTA

Yes, Petruchio.

BIONDELLO

No, I said his horse is coming, with him on its back.

BAPTISTA

Well, that's the same thing.

BIONDELLO

No, by Saint Jamy,
I'll bet you a penny!
A man and his horse
Aren't the same person—
Not that there's much difference.

PETRUCHIO *and* GRUMIO *enter.*

PETRUCHIO

Whoa! Where is everybody?

BAPTISTA

You are welcome, sir.

PETRUCHIO

I don't *feel* well.

BAPTISTA

I don't notice you limping.

TRANIO

(as LUCENTIO*)* And I would like it if you were a bit more formally dressed.

PETRUCHIO
85   Were it better I should rush in thus—
        But where is Kate? Where is my lovely bride?
        How does my father? Gentles, methinks you frown.
        And wherefore gaze this goodly company
        As if they saw some wondrous monument,
90   Some comet or unusual prodigy?

BAPTISTA
        Why, sir, you know this is your wedding day.
        First were we sad, fearing you would not come,
        Now sadder that you come so unprovided.
        Fie, doff this habit, shame to your estate,
95   An eyesore to our solemn festival.

TRANIO
        And tell us what occasion of import
        Hath all so long detained you from your wife
        And sent you hither so unlike yourself.

PETRUCHIO
        Tedious it were to tell and harsh to hear.
100   Sufficeth I am come to keep my word,
        Though in some part enforcèd to digress,
        Which, at more leisure, I will so excuse
        As you shall well be satisfied withal.
        But where is Kate? I stay too long from her.
105   The morning wears. 'Tis time we were at church.

TRANIO
        See not your bride in these unreverent robes.
        Go to my chamber, put on clothes of mine.

PETRUCHIO
        Not I, believe me. Thus I'll visit her.

BAPTISTA
        But thus, I trust, you will not marry her.

PETRUCHIO

Isn't it better this way? But where is Kate? Where is my lovely bride? *(to* BAPTISTA*)* How is my father-in-law? Gentlemen, you seem displeased. What's everyone staring at? You look as if you'd seen something unusual—a comet or something.

BAPTISTA

Why, sir, you know this is your wedding day. First we were sad because we were afraid you wouldn't come. Now we're even sadder to see that you've come so unprepared. For heaven's sake, take off that get-up. It's a disgrace to a man of your social position and an insult to this solemn ceremony.

TRANIO

And tell us what extraordinary occurrence made you so late for your wedding and drove you to present yourself in an outfit that's so—not typical of you.

PETRUCHIO

It's a long story—and tough to listen to. It's enough that I'm here according to my promise, though I will have to deviate from it to some extent—for reasons which, when I explain them later, you'll understand completely. But where is Kate? We're wasting time here. It's getting late and time we were in church.

TRANIO

Don't greet your bride in these disgraceful clothes. Go to my room and put on something of mine.

PETRUCHIO

Not me. I'll see her like this.

BAPTISTA

But surely you're not planning to *marry* her in what you're wearing!

PETRUCHIO

110   Good sooth, even thus. Therefore, ha' done with words:
   To me she's married, not unto my clothes.
   Could I repair what she will wear in me
   As I can change these poor accoutrements,
   'Twere well for Kate and better for myself.
115   But what a fool am I to chat with you,
   When I should bid good morrow to my bride
   And seal the title with a lovely kiss!

Exeunt PETRUCHIO *and* GRUMIO

TRANIO

   He hath some meaning in his mad attire.
   We will persuade him, be it possible,
120   To put on better ere he go to church.

BAPTISTA

   I'll after him, and see the event of this.

Exeunt BAPTISTA, GREMIO, *and attendants*

TRANIO

   But sir, to love concerneth us to add
   Her father's liking, which to bring to pass,
   As I before unparted to your worship,
125   I am to get a man—whate'er he be
   It skills not much, we'll fit him to our turn—
   And he shall be "Vincentio of Pisa"
   And make assurance here in Padua
   Of greater sums than I have promisèd.
130   So shall you quietly enjoy your hope
   And marry sweet Bianca with consent.

PETRUCHIO

Yes, just like this. But enough talk. It's me she's marrying and not my clothes. Though I expect she'll wear me out more quickly than I'll wear out what I'm wearing—which will be good for her and even better for me! But what a fool I am to stand here chatting when I should bid good morning to my bride and seal the bargain with a loving kiss.

PETRUCHIO and GRUMIO exit.

TRANIO

He must be wearing this crazy outfit for some reason. I'll try to persuade him to put on something more appropriate before going to the church, if it's at all possible.

BAPTISTA

I'll go too and make sure that happens.

BAPTISTA, GREMIO, and attendants exit.

TRANIO

But sir, you need to get her father's consent as well as her love. And to that end, as I explained to your worship, I'm looking for a man—any man, it doesn't matter; we'll suit him to our purpose—who can pretend to be your father, Vincentio. And *he'll* guarantee the dowry—for even more money than I've promised on your behalf. This way, you'll get your wish and marry sweet Bianca with her father's consent and with the least possible hassle.

LUCENTIO
　　Were it not that my fellow schoolmaster
　　Doth watch Bianca's steps so narrowly,
　　'Twere good, methinks, to steal our marriage,
135　　Which, once performed, let all the world say no,
　　I'll keep mine own despite of all the world.

TRANIO
　　That by degrees we mean to look into
　　And watch our vantage in this business.
　　We'll overreach the graybeard, Gremio,
140　　The narrow-prying father, Minola,
　　The quaint musician, amorous Litio,
　　All for my master's sake, Lucentio.

Enter GREMIO

　　Signior Gremio, came you from the church?

GREMIO
　　As willingly as e'er I came from school.

TRANIO
145　　*(as* LUCENTIO*)* And is the bride and bridegroom coming
　　home?

GREMIO
　　A bridegroom, say you? 'Tis a groom indeed,
　　A grumbling groom, and that the girl shall find.

TRANIO
　　(as LUCENTIO*)* Curster than she? Why, 'tis impossible.

GREMIO
150　　Why, he's a devil, a devil, a very fiend.

TRANIO
　　(as LUCENTIO*)* Why, she's a devil, a devil, the devil's dam.

LUCENTIO

If my fellow schoolmaster weren't keeping such a close watch on her, I'd think about eloping. Then it wouldn't matter what anyone said—I'd keep what's mine, whatever the rest of the world said.

TRANIO

Don't worry, I'm looking into that too. I'm on top of the situation—monitoring it very closely. We'll outwit them all—that old geezer, Gremio; the suspicious father, Minola; the prim musician lover, Litio—all for the sake of my master, Lucentio.

GREMIO *enters.*

Signior Gremio, are you coming from the church?

GREMIO

As eagerly as I ever came from school.

TRANIO

(speaking as LUCENTIO*)* And will the bride and bridegroom be here soon?

GREMIO

Bridegroom? This guy is more like the groom who cleans the stable—a grumbling groom at that, as the poor girl is discovering.

TRANIO

(speaking as LUCENTIO*)* You mean he's worse than she is? That's not possible!

GREMIO

No, he's a devil—a devil, I tell you! An utter fiend.

TRANIO

(speaking as LUCENTIO*)* No, *she's* a devil—a devil, I tell you. The devil's grandmother.

GREMIO

Tut, she's a lamb, a dove, a fool to him!
I'll tell you, Sir Lucentio: when the priest
Should ask if Katherine should be his wife,
155 "Ay, by gogs wouns!" quoth he, and swore so loud
That, all amazed, the priest let fall the book,
And as he stooped again to take it up,
The mad-brained bridegroom took him such a cuff
That down fell priest and book, and book and priest.
160 "Now take them up," quoth he, "if any list."

TRANIO

(as LUCENTIO*)* What said the wench when he rose again?

GREMIO

Trembled and shook, for why he stamped and swore
As if the vicar meant to cozen him.
But after many ceremonies done,
165 He calls for wine. "A health!" quoth he, as if
He had been aboard, carousing to his mates
After a storm; quaffed off the muscatel
And threw the sops all in the sexton's face,
Having no other reason
170 But that his beard grew thin and hungerly
And seemed to ask him sops as he was drinking.
This done, he took the bride about the neck
And kissed her lips with such a clamorous smack
That at the parting all the church did echo.
175 And I, seeing this, came thence for very shame,
And after me, I know, the rout is coming.
Such a mad marriage never was before.

Music

Hark, hark! I hear the minstrels play.

GREMIO

Why, she's a lamb, a dove, a child compared to him! Picture this: when the priest asked Katherine if she would have him, he answered, "Hell, yes!" and swore so loud that the priest drops the prayer book. Everyone froze, and as the priest stooped to pick it up again the lunatic bridegroom smacked him so hard that the priest and book went flying! *Then* he said, "Now pick them up—if anyone dares."

TRANIO

(as LUCENTIO) What did the girl say when the priest got up?

GREMIO

She trembled and shook because he stamped and swore and carried on as though the vicar were trying to put something over on him. Finally, the ceremony done, he called for wine. "A health!" he shouted, like some sailor aboard ship, carousing with his mates after a storm. Then he chugs the wine and throws the dregs in the sexton's face. Why? Because the fellow's beard looked thin, he said, and it seemed to be asking him for the dregs while he was drinking. Next he slung his arm around the bride's neck and kissed her with such a smack that when they parted the sound of their lips made the whole church echo. That was the limit for me. I got out of there as fast as I could. I know the rest of the crowd isn't far behind me. It's disgraceful! You never saw such a mockery of a marriage in your life!

Music plays.

There go the minstrels. They've started up.

Enter PETRUCHIO, KATHERINE, BIANCA, BAPTISTA,
HORTENSIO, GRUMIO, *and train*

PETRUCHIO
Gentlemen and friends, I thank you for your pains.
180 I know you think to dine with me today
And have prepared great store of wedding cheer,
But so it is, my haste doth call me hence,
And therefore here I mean to take my leave.

BAPTISTA
Is 't possible you will away tonight?

PETRUCHIO
185 I must away today, before night come.
Make it no wonder. If you knew my business,
You would entreat me rather go than stay.
And, honest company, I thank you all,
That have beheld me give away myself
190 To this most patient, sweet and virtuous wife.
Dine with my father, drink a health to me,
For I must hence, and farewell to you all.

TRANIO
(as LUCENTIO*)* Let us entreat you stay till after dinner.

PETRUCHIO
It may not be.

GREMIO
Let me entreat you.

PETRUCHIO
195 It cannot be.

KATHERINE
Let me entreat you.

PETRUCHIO
I am content.

KATHERINE
Are you content to stay?

> PETRUCHIO *and* KATHERINE *enter, with* BIANCA, BAPTISTA, HORTENSIO, GRUMIO, *and members of the wedding procession.*

PETRUCHIO

Gentlemen and friends, thanks for bothering to come. I know you expected me to stay to dinner and have prepared a celebratory feast, but as it happens I'm called away. So let me say goodbye.

BAPTISTA

You're not thinking of leaving tonight, surely?

PETRUCHIO

Not tonight—today. If you knew the reason, you'd understand and would urge me to go rather than stay. Good friends, I thank you all for coming to see me wed this patient, sweet, virtuous wife. Dine with my father and drink a health to me. I have to leave. Goodbye to you all.

TRANIO

(as LUCENTIO*)* Please, stay till after dinner.

PETRUCHIO

Can't do it.

GREMIO

As a favor to *me?*

PETRUCHIO

Nope.

KATHERINE

As a favor to *me?*

PETRUCHIO

I'm delighted.

KATHERINE

Delighted to stay?

PETRUCHIO
I am content you shall entreat me stay,
But yet not stay, entreat me how you can.

KATHERINE
200   Now, if you love me, stay.

PETRUCHIO
                              Grumio, my horse.

GRUMIO
Ay, sir, they be ready. The oats have eaten the horses.

KATHERINE
Nay, then,
Do what thou canst, I will not go today,
No, nor tomorrow, not till I please myself.
205   The door is open, sir. There lies your way.
You may be jogging whiles your boots are green.
For me, I'll not be gone till I please myself.
'Tis like you'll prove a jolly surly groom,
That take it on you at the first so roundly.

PETRUCHIO
210   O Kate, content thee. Prithee, be not angry.

KATHERINE
I will be angry. What hast thou to do?—
Father, be quiet. He shall stay my leisure.

GREMIO
Ay, marry, sir, now it begins to work.

KATHERINE
Gentlemen, forward to the bridal dinner.
215   I see a woman may be made a fool
If she had not a spirit to resist.

PETRUCHIO
They shall go forward, Kate, at thy command.—
Obey the bride, you that attend on her.
Go to the feast, revel and domineer,
220   Carouse full measure to her maidenhead,
Be mad and merry, or go hang yourselves.
But for my bonny Kate, she must with me.

PETRUCHIO

Delighted to hear you ask so nicely, but I won't stay in any case.

KATHERINE

Look, if you love me, stay.

PETRUCHIO

Grumio, get me my horse.

GRUMIO

Yes, sir, they're ready. They've eaten themselves sick.

KATHERINE

All right, then, do what you like. I won't leave today. Not tomorrow, either. I'll leave when I'm good and ready. The door is open, sir. Feel free to use it. Go on, wear your boots out! As for me, I'll leave when I like. If you're this high-handed to start with, I can imagine how arrogant and arbitrary you'll be as a husband.

PETRUCHIO

Calm down, Kate. Please don't be angry.

KATHERINE

I will be angry. What business is it of yours?—Father, be quiet. He'll stay as long as I say.

GREMIO

Okay, now it starts!

KATHERINE

Gentlemen, on to the bridal dinner. I see a woman may be made a fool of if she doesn't have nerve enough to stand up for herself.

PETRUCHIO

They *shall* go in to the bridal dinner, Kate—they're yours to command. Obey the bride, guests! Go to the banquet: revel, feast, and carouse! Drink yourselves silly toasting her virginity! Be wild and merry—or go to hell. But as for my bonny Kate, she must come with me. No, don't puff out your chests and stamp and

Nay, look not big, nor stamp, nor stare, nor fret;
I will be master of what is mine own.
225 She is my goods, my chattels; she is my house,
My household stuff, my field, my barn,
My horse, my ox, my ass, my anything.
And here she stands, touch her whoever dare.
I'll bring mine action on the proudest he
230 That stops my way in Padua.—Grumio,
Draw forth thy weapon, we are beset with thieves.
Rescue thy mistress if thou be a man.—
Fear not, sweet wench, they shall not touch thee, Kate.
I'll buckler thee against a million.

Exeunt PETRUCHIO, KATHERINE, *and* GRUMIO

BAPTISTA
235 Nay, let them go, a couple of quiet ones.

GREMIO
Went they not quickly, I should die with laughing.

TRANIO
(as LUCENTIO*)* Of all mad matches never was the like.

LUCENTIO
(as CAMBIO*)* Mistress, what's your opinion of your sister?

BIANCA
That, being mad herself, she's madly mated.

GREMIO
240 I warrant him, Petruchio is Kated.

BAPTISTA
Neighbors and friends, though bride and bridegroom wants
For to supply the places at the table,
You know there wants no junkets at the feast.

stare wonderingly. I will be master of what belongs to me. She is my property, one of my possessions—just like my house and everything in it, and my field, my barn, my horse, my ox, my donkey—anything of mine you care to name. Here she is; I dare you to touch her! I'll sue anyone in Padua who tries to stand in my way, no matter how powerful he is.—Grumio, draw your sword! We are surrounded by thieves. Rescue your mistress! Prove yourself a man! Don't be afraid, sweet girl, I won't let them touch you. I'll protect you, Kate, against a million of them.

PETRUCHIO, KATHERINE, *and* GRUMIO *exit.*

BAPTISTA

No, let them go. They're certainly a peaceful couple!

GREMIO

If they hadn't left soon, I would have died laughing.

TRANIO

(as LUCENTIO*)* Of all the mad matches, this is by far the craziest.

LUCENTIO

(as CAMBIO*)* Mistress, what's your opinion of your sister?

BIANCA

That since she's mad herself, she's married a madman.

GREMIO

I guarantee you, Petruchio's going to suffer from his Kate.

BAPTISTA

Neighbors and friends, though we don't have anyone for the bride and bridegroom's places at the table, you know there's nothing missing in the feast itself.

(to TRANIO*)*
Lucentio, you shall supply the bridegroom's place,
245   And let Bianca take her sister's room.

TRANIO
(as LUCENTIO*)* Shall sweet Bianca practice how to bride it?

BAPTISTA
She shall, Lucentio. Come, gentlemen, let's go.

Exeunt

(to TRANIO*)* Lucentio, you shall assume the bridegroom's place and let Bianca take her sister's seat.

TRANIO

(as LUCENTIO*)* Shall sweet Bianca practice how to be a bride?

BAPTISTA

She shall, Lucentio. Come, gentlemen, let's go in.

They all exit.

ACT FOUR
SCENE 1

Enter GRUMIO

GRUMIO
Fie, fie on all tired jades, on all mad masters, and all foul
ways! Was ever man so beaten? Was ever man so 'rayed?
Was ever man so weary? I am sent before to make a fire, and
they are coming after to warm them. Now, were not I a little
pot and soon hot, my very lips might freeze to my teeth, my
tongue to the roof of my mouth, my heart in my belly, ere I
should come by a fire to thaw me. But I with blowing the fire
shall warm myself. For, considering the weather, a taller
man than I will take cold.—Holla, ho! Curtis!

Enter CURTIS

CURTIS
Who is that calls so coldly?

GRUMIO
A piece of ice. If thou doubt it, thou mayst slide from my
shoulder to my heel with no greater a run but my head and
my neck. A fire, good Curtis.

CURTIS
Is my master and his wife coming, Grumio?

GRUMIO
Oh, ay, Curtis, ay, and therefore fire, fire. Cast on no water.

CURTIS
Is she so hot a shrew as she's reported?

ACT FOUR
SCENE 1

GRUMIO *enters.*

GRUMIO

To hell with all worn-out horses, all crazy masters, and all bad roads. Was a man ever beaten as much as me? Was a man ever as dirty as me? Was a man ever so tired? I have been sent on ahead to light a fire, and they are coming after to warm themselves. It's a good thing I'm like a little pot and warm up quickly, or else my lips themselves would freeze and stick to my teeth, my tongue to the roof of my mouth, and my heart would freeze in my belly, before I managed to get thawed out. I'll warm myself by blowing on the fire. A taller man than I would catch cold in weather like this. Hey! Curtis! Hello!

CURTIS *enters.*

CURTIS

Who calls so coldly?

GRUMIO

A piece of ice. Trust me, you could slide all the way from my shoulder to my heel taking no more of a running start than the distance between my head and my neck. Start the fire, good Curtis.

CURTIS

Are my master and his wife coming, Grumio?

GRUMIO

Yes, yes, Curtis, so hurry up and start the fire. Leave out the water.

CURTIS

Is she as fiery a shrew as they say?

GRUMIO
She was, good Curtis, before this frost. But thou knowest
winter tames man, woman and beast, for it hath tamed my
old master and my new mistress and myself, fellow Curtis.

CURTIS
20   Away, you three-inch fool! I am no beast.

GRUMIO
Am I but three inches? Why, thy horn is a foot, and so long
am I, at the least. But wilt thou make a fire, or shall I
complain on thee to our mistress, whose hand, she being
now at hand, thou shalt soon feel, to thy cold comfort, for
25   being slow in thy hot office?

CURTIS
I prithee, good Grumio, tell me, how goes the world?

GRUMIO
A cold world, Curtis, in every office but thine, and
therefore fire! Do thy duty, and have thy duty, for my
master and mistress are almost frozen to death.

CURTIS
30   There's fire ready. And therefore, good Grumio, the news.

GRUMIO
Why, "Jack, boy! Ho, boy!" and as much news as wilt thou.

CURTIS
Come, you are so full of cony-catching!

GRUMIO
Why, therefore fire, for I have caught extreme cold.
Where's the cook? Is supper ready, the house trimmed,
35   rushes strewed, cobwebs swept, the servingmen in their
new fustian, their white stockings, and every officer his
wedding garment on? Be the Jacks fair within, the Jills fair
without, the carpets laid, and everything in order?

GRUMIO

Well she was, good Curtis, before this frost. But you know how winter tames man, woman, and beast. And it's tamed my old master and my new mistress and myself, my good colleague.

CURTIS

Who are you calling "beast," midget. You're no bigger than three inches!

GRUMIO

Three inches? Really? Your horn is a foot long, and I'm at least that size. Now are you going to make a fire, or am I going to have to report you to our mistress, whose hand, now that she is herself at hand, you'll be feeling soon. You'll find it cold comfort, but that's what you get for being slow with your warming duties.

CURTIS

So tell me, Grumio, how goes the world?

GRUMIO

Cold, Curtis. It's a cold world, except for people who have to start fires. Therefore, do your duty and take your reward, because my master and mistress are nearly frozen to death.

CURTIS

The fire is ready. So go on, tell me the news.

GRUMIO

Grumio's response is a line from a song.

"Why, Jack boy, ho boy!" and all the news you want.

CURTIS

Oh, you're just *so* funny.

GRUMIO

Well, make a fire, then. I think I'm getting delirious. Where's the cook? Is supper ready? Is the house fixed up, the floor covered, the cobwebs swept out of the corners, the servingmen in their new work clothes and the household servants each in his wedding suit? Are all the cups and glasses in their places, the tablecloths laid out—everything in order?

CURTIS
All ready. And therefore, I pray thee, news.

GRUMIO
40   First, know my horse is tired, my master and mistress fallen
out.

CURTIS
How?

GRUMIO
Out of their saddles into the dirt, and thereby hangs a tale.

CURTIS
Let's ha' 't, good Grumio.

GRUMIO
45   Lend thine ear.

CURTIS
Here.

GRUMIO
There!

Strikes him

CURTIS
This 'tis to feel a tale, not to hear a tale.

GRUMIO
And therefore 'tis called a sensible tale. And this cuff was
50   but to knock at your ear and beseech list'ning. Now I begin:
Imprimis, we came down a foul hill, my master riding
behind my mistress—

CURTIS
Both of one horse?

GRUMIO
What's that to thee?

CURTIS

Everything's ready. So tell me what's been going on.

GRUMIO

Well, first of all, my horse is tired and my master and mistress have had a falling out.

CURTIS

How?

GRUMIO

From their saddles into the dirt—but that's another story.

CURTIS

Well, let's have it, Grumio.

GRUMIO

Lean forward.

CURTIS

Here.

GRUMIO

There!

GRUMIO *strikes* CURTIS.

CURTIS

This is to feel the news, not hear it.

GRUMIO

That's what makes it "sensitive" news. I was just knocking to see if anyone was home. Now, I'll begin: first, we came down a steep hill, my master riding behind my mistress—

CURTIS

Both on one horse?

GRUMIO

What's the difference?

CURTIS

55   Why, a horse.

GRUMIO

Tell thou the tale! But hadst thou not crossed me, thou
shouldst have heard how her horse fell, and she under her
horse. Thou shouldst have heard in how miry a place, how
she was bemoiled, how he left her with the horse upon her,

60   how he beat me because her horse stumbled, how she
waded through the dirt to pluck him off me, how he swore,
how she prayed that never prayed before, how I cried, how
the horses ran away, how her bridle was burst, how I lost my
crupper, with many things of worthy memory which now

65   shall die in oblivion, and thou return unexperienced to thy
grave.

CURTIS

By this reck'ning he is more shrew than she.

GRUMIO

Ay, and that thou and the proudest of you all shall find
when he comes home. But what talk I of this? Call forth

70   Nathaniel, Joseph, Nicholas, Philip, Walter, Sugarsop, and
the rest. Let their heads be slickly combed, their blue coats
brushed, and their garters of an indifferent knit. Let them
curtsy with their left legs, and not presume to touch a hair
of my master's horse-tail till they kiss their hands. Are they

75   all ready?

CURTIS

They are.

GRUMIO

Call them forth.

CURTIS

(calling offstage) Do you hear, ho? you must meet my
master to countenance my mistress.

CURTIS

Well, the difference of a horse!

GRUMIO

Oh, tell it yourself if you're so smart. It's too bad. If you hadn't made me angry, you would have heard all about how her horse fell with her under it, how swampy the place was, too, and how she was covered in mud, and how he left her like that, with the horse on top of her, and how he beat *me* because *her* horse stumbled, and how she waded through the dirt to pull him off me, and how he swore, how she prayed—this woman who never prayed before—and how I yelled, and how the horses ran away, and how her bridle broke, and how I lost my riding crop, and many other things worth telling, which now will all be lost to memory, and you'll go to your grave ignorant.

CURTIS

By the sound of it, he's a bigger shrew than she is.

GRUMIO

Yes—as you and the rest will find out as soon as he's home. But why am I telling you this? Get them in here—Nathaniel, Joseph, Nicholas, Philip, Walter, Sugarsop, and the rest. Tell them to slick down their hair, brush their blue coats, and make sure their socks match. Have them click their heels together and don't dare touch a hair of the master's horse's tail till they kiss their hands. Are they all ready?

CURTIS

They are.

GRUMIO

Get them in here.

CURTIS

(calling offstage) Hey! Does anyone hear me? Hey! You have to come and greet the master and face the new mistress.

GRUMIO
80   Why, she hath a face of her own.

CURTIS
Who knows not that?

GRUMIO
Thou, it seems, that calls for company to countenance her.

CURTIS
I call them forth to credit her.

GRUMIO
Why, she comes to borrow nothing of them.

Enter four or five Servingmen

NATHANIEL
85   Welcome home, Grumio.

PHILIP
How now, Grumio?

JOSEPH
What, Grumio!

NICHOLAS
Fellow Grumio!

NATHANIEL
How now, old lad?

GRUMIO
90   Welcome, you!—How now, you?—What, you!—Fellow,
you!—And thus much for greeting. Now, my spruce
companions, is all ready, and all things neat?

NATHANIEL
All things is ready. How near is our master?

GRUMIO
E'en at hand, alighted by this. And therefore be not—
95   Cock's passion, silence! I hear my master.

Enter PETRUCHIO *and* KATHERINE

GRUMIO

She already has a face.

CURTIS

Yeah, so?

GRUMIO

You just said they had to face her.

CURTIS

I meant they had to give her credit.

GRUMIO

She's not going to borrow money from them.

Four or five servants enter.

NATHANIEL

Welcome home, Grumio.

PHILIP

What's up, Grumio?

JOSEPH

Hey, Grumio!

NICHOLAS

My man Grumio!

NATHANIEL

So what's the story, old boy?

GRUMIO

Welcome yourself!—What's up with *you?*—Hey to *you!*—So much for greetings. Now, my well-dressed friends, is everything ready and in order?

NATHANIEL

Everything's ready. How soon will the master be here?

GRUMIO

Any minute. Probably here already. So be careful, and don't—God! Quiet, I hear him coming.

PETRUCHIO *and* KATHERINE *enter.*

PETRUCHIO
Where be these knaves? What, no man at door
To hold my stirrup nor to take my horse!
Where is Nathaniel, Gregory, Philip?

ALL SERVINGMEN
Here, here, sir! Here, sir!

PETRUCHIO
100   "Here, sir! Here, sir! Here, sir! Here, sir!"
You loggerheaded and unpolished grooms!
What, no attendance? No regard? No duty?
Where is the foolish knave I sent before?

GRUMIO
Here, sir, as foolish as I was before.

PETRUCHIO
105   You peasant swain! You whoreson malt-horse drudge!
Did I not bid thee meet me in the park
And bring along these rascal knaves with thee?

GRUMIO
Nathaniel's coat, sir, was not fully made,
And Gabriel's pumps were all unpinked i' th' heel.
110   There was no link to color Peter's hat,
And Walter's dagger was not come from sheathing.
There were none fine but Adam, Rafe, and Gregory.
The rest were ragged, old, and beggarly.
Yet, as they are, here are they come to meet you.

PETRUCHIO
115   Go, rascals, go, and fetch my supper in.

                                                                    Exeunt Servants

Singing
Where is the life that late I led—
*Where are those—*Sit down, Kate, and welcome.—
Soud, soud, soud, soud!

Enter Servants with supper

PETRUCHIO

Where are those bastards? Where is the boy who's supposed to help me get off my horse and take him to the stable? Where is Nathaniel? Where's Gregory? Where's Philip?

ALL SERVANTS

Here, here, sir! Here, sir!

PETRUCHIO

"Here, sir! Here, sir! Here, sir! Here, sir!" You stupid, unpolished dolts! I get no service, no respect, no attention! Where is the fool I sent on ahead?

GRUMIO

Here, sir, as foolish as ever.

PETRUCHIO

You unwashed farmworker! You bastard workhorse drudge! Didn't I tell you to meet me outside and bring these morons with you?

GRUMIO

Nathaniel's coat was being fixed, sir. And one of Gabriel's shoes had a broken heel. And Peter couldn't find a matching hat. And Walter couldn't get his dagger out of its sheath. Only Adam, Rafe, and Gregory were ready. The rest were just a mess—but such as they are, sir, they're here to welcome you.

PETRUCHIO

Go, blockheads, go, and bring my supper to me.

The servants exit.

(singing) Where is the life I led until recently? Where are those—Sit down, Kate, make yourself at home.—Come on, come on, come on, come on.

Servants enter with supper.

Why, when, I say?—Nay, good sweet Kate, be merry.—
120   Off with my boots, you rogues! You villains, when?

Sings

It was the friar of orders gray,
As he forth walkèd on his way:—

A servant tries to take off PETRUCHIO*'s boots.*

Out, you rogue! You pluck my foot awry.
Take that, and mend the plucking off the other.

Strikes him

125   Be merry, Kate.—Some water, here, what, ho!
Where's my spaniel Troilus? Sirrah, get you hence
And bid my cousin Ferdinand come hither.

Exit a servant

One, Kate, that you must kiss and be acquainted with.—
Where are my slippers? Shall I have some water?—

Enter one with water

130   Come, Kate, and wash, and welcome heartily.—
You whoreson villain! Will you let it fall?

Strikes him

KATHERINE
Patience, I pray you! 'Twas a fault unwilling.

Did I say later? I said *now!*—Smile, Kate! Be happy.—
Get my boots off, you apes! You idiots, *now!*

*(singing) It was a friar in robes of gray, who walked
along the road one day:—(a servant tries to take off*
PETRUCHIO's *boots)* Stop, you moron! You're twisting
my foot! Take that, and see you do a better job with the
other one. *(he strikes the servant)* Be happy, Kate!—
Bring me some water! Where's my spaniel Troilus?
Hey boy, go tell my cousin Ferdinand to get in here.

A servant exits.

You'll love this guy, Kate—anyway, you'd better!
Where are my slippers? Can we have some water
please here?—

A servant enters with water.

Come and wash, Kate, make yourself at home. Son of
a bitch, you spilled it! *(he strikes the servant)*

KATHERINE
Take it easy! Please! It was just an accident!

PETRUCHIO
    A whoreson, beetle-headed, flap-eared knave!—
    Come, Kate, sit down. I know you have a stomach.
135   Will you give thanks, sweet Kate, or else shall I?—
    What's this? Mutton?

FIRST SERVANT
    Ay.

PETRUCHIO
        Who brought it?

PETER
                  I.

PETRUCHIO
    'Tis burnt, and so is all the meat.
    What dogs are these! Where is the rascal cook?
140   How durst you, villains, bring it from the dresser
    And serve it thus to me that love it not?
    There, take it to you, trenchers, cups, and all!

Throws the meat, & c. about the stage

    You heedless joltheads and unmannered slaves!
    What, do you grumble? I'll be with you straight.

Exeunt servants

KATHERINE
145   I pray you, husband, be not so disquiet.
    The meat was well, if you were so contented.

PETRUCHIO
    I tell thee, Kate, 'twas burnt and dried away.
    And I expressly am forbid to touch it,
    For it engenders choler, planteth anger;
150   And better 'twere that both of us did fast,
    Since of ourselves, ourselves are choleric,
    Than feed it with such over-roasted flesh.
    Be patient, tomorrow 't shall be mended,
    And, for this night, we'll fast for company.

PETRUCHIO

> He's a son of a bitch, a moron, a total jerk.—Come sit down, Kate, I know you must be hungry. Will you say grace, sweet Kate, or shall I?—What is this? Mutton?

FIRST SERVANT

> Yes.

PETRUCHIO

> Who brought it out here?

PETER

> I did.

PETRUCHIO

> It's burnt. The whole thing is burnt. You bastards! Where is that moron of a cook? You devils! How dare you serve it to me this way! There, take it all back— plates, cups, the whole thing. *(throws the meat and everything else around the stage)* You careless block-heads and unwashed slaves! I heard that! I'll deal with you in a minute.

> *Servants exit.*

KATHERINE

> Please, dear, calm down. The meat was fine if you wanted to eat it.

PETRUCHIO

> And I'm telling you it was burnt and dried out. I'm not allowed to eat overcooked meat. It gives me indigestion and that makes me irritable. Very, very irritable. Better for us to go hungry, since we're both hotheaded, than for us to eat meat that's been cooked too long. But don't worry, tomorrow it will get straightened out. Tonight we'll go without food.

Overcooked meat was thought to produce choler, one of the four humors—the one that gave rise to anger.

155   Come, I will bring thee to thy bridal chamber.

Exeunt

Enter Servants severally

NATHANIEL
        Peter, didst ever see the like?

PETER
        He kills her in her own humor.

Enter CURTIS

GRUMIO
        Where is he?

CURTIS
        In her chamber,
160   Making a sermon of continency to her,
        And rails and swears and rates, that she, poor soul,
        Knows not which way to stand, to look, to speak,
        And sits as one new-risen from a dream.
        Away, away, for he is coming hither!

Exeunt

Enter PETRUCHIO

PETRUCHIO
165   Thus have I politicly begun my reign,
        And 'tis my hope to end successfully.
        My falcon now is sharp and passing empty,
        And, till she stoop, she must not be full-gorged,
        For then she never looks upon her lure.
170   Another way I have to man my haggard,
        To make her come and know her keeper's call.

Come, I'll show you your bridal chamber.

They exit.

Servants enter from different parts of the stage.

NATHANIEL

Peter, did you ever see anything like it?

PETER

He's giving her a taste of her own medicine.

CURTIS enters.

GRUMIO

Where is he?

CURTIS

In her room, lecturing her on the virtues of self-control. He rants and rails and swears and she, poor thing, doesn't know how to stand or look or speak. She sits like a person who's just woken up from a dream. Look out, he's coming!

They exit.

PETRUCHIO enters.

PETRUCHIO

Well, I've begun my reign with a carefully thought-out plan, and I have every hope of succeeding. My falcon is now hungry and unfed and must not be given enough to eat until she comes to me, for if her hunger is satisfied, she'll pay no attention to the bait. I have another plan to make my bird come to me and recognize her owner's call is to keep her from sleeping—

That is, to watch her, as we watch these kites
That bate and beat and will not be obedient.
She ate no meat today, nor none shall eat.
175 Last night she slept not, nor tonight she shall not.
As with the meat, some undeservèd fault
I'll find about the making of the bed,
And here I'll fling the pillow, there the bolster,
This way the coverlet, another way the sheets.
180 Ay, and amid this hurly I intend
That all is done in reverend care of her.
And, in conclusion, she shall watch all night,
And if she chance to nod I'll rail and brawl,
And with the clamor keep her still awake.
185 This is a way to kill a wife with kindness,
And thus I'll curb her mad and headstrong humor.
He that knows better how to tame a shrew,
Now let him speak; 'tis charity to show.

Exit

the way trainers do with young hawks that flutter and flap and will not obey. She had no food today and will have none. Last night she got no sleep, and she won't get any tonight. Just as I did with the meat, I'll make up some problem with the way the bed is made, and throw the pillow one way and the cushion the other, and the blanket over here and the sheets over there. And through all the shouting and fuss, I'll swear that it's all out of love for her. The end result will be that she'll sit up all night. And if she starts to drop off, I'll rant and yell until I wake her up . This is how to kill a wife with kindness. And this way I'll cure her wild and willful nature. If anyone here knows a better way to tame a shrew, speak up, please. It would be much appreciated.

He exits.

ACT 4, SCENE 2

Enter TRANIO *as* LUCENTIO *and* HORTENSIO *as* LITIO

TRANIO
(*as* LUCENTIO)
Is 't possible, friend Litio, that mistress Bianca
Doth fancy any other but Lucentio?
I tell you, sir, she bears me fair in hand.

HORTENSIO
(*as* LITIO) Sir, to satisfy you in what I have said,
5   Stand by and mark the manner of his teaching.
They stand aside

Enter BIANCA *and* LUCENTIO *as* CAMBIO

LUCENTIO
(*as* CAMBIO) Now, mistress, profit you in what you read?

BIANCA
What, master, read you? First resolve me that.

LUCENTIO
(*as* CAMBIO) I read that I profess, *The Art to Love.*

BIANCA
And may you prove, sir, master of your art.

LUCENTIO
10   (*as* CAMBIO) While you, sweet dear, prove mistress of my
heart!

HORTENSIO
(*as* LITIO) Quick proceeders, marry! Now, tell me, I pray,
You that durst swear that your mistress Bianca
Loved none in the world so well as Lucentio.

TRANIO
15   (*as* LUCENTIO) O despiteful love! Unconstant womankind!
I tell thee, Litio, this is wonderful!

ACT 4, SCENE 2

TRANIO *enters, disguised as* LUCENTIO, *accompanied by* HORTENSIO, *disguised as* LITIO.

TRANIO

(*as* LUCENTIO) I don't believe it, Litio. It's not possible that Bianca could prefer another man to me. I've seen the way she behaves.

HORTENSIO

(*as* LITIO) You want proof of what I'm telling you? Stand right here and watch this fellow's "lesson." (*they stand off to one side*)

BIANCA *enters with* LUCENTIO *disguised as* CAMBIO.

LUCENTIO

(*as* CAMBIO) Well, mistress, are you learning from what you're reading?

BIANCA

What are you reading, teacher? Answer me that first.

LUCENTIO

Ovid's The Art of Love was a manual of seduction.

(*as* CAMBIO) I'm reading the book I know best—*The Art of Love.*

BIANCA

I hope you're an expert in your field.

LUCENTIO

(*as* CAMBIO) Well, my dear, you're the mistress of my heart in any case!

HORTENSIO

(*as* LITIO) Quick work for schoolwork! How do you explain that? I though you said your precious Bianca loved no one better than you, Lucentio!

TRANIO

(*as* LUCENTIO) Oh spiteful love! Faithless womanhood! It's incredible, Litio!

HORTENSIO
Mistake no more. I am not Litio,
Nor a musician as I seem to be,
But one that scorn to live in this disguise
20   For such a one as leaves a gentleman
And makes a god of such a cullion.
Know, sir, that I am called Hortensio.

TRANIO
(as LUCENTIO*)* Signior Hortensio, I have often heard
Of your entire affection to Bianca,
25   And since mine eyes are witness of her lightness,
I will with you, if you be so contented,
Forswear Bianca and her love for ever.

HORTENSIO
See how they kiss and court! Signior Lucentio,
Here is my hand, and here I firmly vow
30   Never to woo her more, but do forswear her
As one unworthy all the former favors
That I have fondly flattered her withal.

TRANIO
And here I take the like unfeignèd oath
Never to marry with her, though she would entreat.
35   Fie on her! See how beastly she doth court him!

HORTENSIO
Would all the world but he had quite forsworn!
For me, that I may surely keep mine oath,
I will be married to a wealthy widow,
Ere three days pass, which hath as long loved me
40   As I have loved this proud disdainful haggard.
And so farewell, Signior Lucentio.
Kindness in women, not their beauteous looks,
Shall win my love, and so I take my leave,
In resolution as I swore before.

Exit

HORTENSIO

Let me come clean. I'm not really Litio. I'm not even a musician, really. In fact, I refuse to go on with this charade for a woman who would choose a lower-class guy like this over a gentleman of my stature. My name is Hortensio, sir.

TRANIO

(as LUCENTIO) Signior Hortensio, I've often heard of your total devotion to Bianca. So, now that I've seen with my own eyes proof of her worthlessness, I'm willing to join you in swearing her off for good, if you like.

HORTENSIO

Look how they kiss and carry on! Signior Lucentio, it's a deal. I hereby swear to have nothing more to do with this girl. I formally declare her unworthy of all the attention and expense I have wasted on her.

TRANIO

And I hereby make the same promise—never to marry her, not even if she begs me. The hell with her! Look how she carries on with him! It's revolting!

HORTENSIO

I wish all her lovers had given her up. Well, to be on the safe side—so I don't go back on my promise—I plan to get myself married to a wealthy widow within the next three days. She's been after me for years—the way I've been for this proud, haughty hag. Farewell, then, Signior Lucentio. From now on, goodness in women, not superficial beauty, will win my heart. I bid you all goodbye. I've made up my mind, and I'm going to stick to it.

He exits.

TRANIO

45   Mistress Bianca, bless you with such grace
As 'longeth to a lover's blessèd case!
Nay, I have ta'en you napping, gentle love,
And have forsworn you with Hortensio.

BIANCA

Tranio, you jest. But have you both forsworn me?

TRANIO

50   Mistress, we have.

LUCENTIO

                  Then we are rid of Litio.

TRANIO

I' faith, he'll have a lusty widow now
That shall be wooed and wedded in a day.

BIANCA

God give him joy!

TRANIO

Ay, and he'll tame her.

BIANCA

55   He says so, Tranio?

TRANIO

Faith, he is gone unto the taming school.

BIANCA

The taming school? What, is there such a place?

TRANIO

Ay, mistress, and Petruchio is the master,
That teacheth tricks eleven and twenty long
60   To tame a shrew and charm her chattering tongue.

Enter **BIONDELLO**

TRANIO

Miss Bianca, may you be blessed with all the happiness you deserve. No, I've caught you out, my dear. You're busted. Hortensio and I have given you up.

BIANCA

You can't mean it, Tranio! Have you both really given me up?

TRANIO

Yes, ma'am, we have.

LUCENTIO

So Litio's out of the picture.

TRANIO

He's going after a young widow. He says he'll court and win her in a day.

BIANCA

Well, good for him!

TRANIO

Yeah, and he's going to tame her.

BIANCA

Is that what he says?

TRANIO

Yep. He's gone to study at the taming school.

BIANCA

The taming school? Is there such a place?

TRANIO

Yes, ma'am. Petruchio runs it. There he teaches piles of tricks for taming a shrew *and* her tongue.

BIONDELLO *enters.*

BIONDELLO
> O master, master, I have watched so long
> That I am dog-weary, but at last I spied
> An ancient angel coming down the hill
> Will serve the turn.

TRANIO
>   What is he, Biondello?

BIONDELLO
65 > Master, a marcantant, or a pedant,
> I know not what, but formal in apparel,
> In gait and countenance surely like a father.

LUCENTIO
> And what of him, Tranio?

TRANIO
> If he be credulous and trust my tale,
70 > I'll make him glad to seem Vincentio
> And give assurance to Baptista Minola
> As if he were the right Vincentio.
> Take in your love, and then let me alone.

Exeunt LUCENTIO *and* BIANCA

Enter a MERCHANT

MERCHANT
> God save you, sir.

TRANIO
> (*as* LUCENTIO)
>   And you, sir. You are welcome.
75 > Travel you far on, or are you at the farthest?

MERCHANT
> Sir, at the farthest for a week or two,
> But then up farther, and as far as Rome,
> And so to Tripoli, if God lend me life.

BIONDELLO

> Master, master, I've been on the lookout so long, I'm ready to fall down dead—but I've got one, finally! There's a trustworthy old fellow coming down the hill who will do the job.

TRANIO

> What does he look like, Biondello?

BIONDELLO

> A merchant or a schoolmaster, sir. Well, I don't know exactly, but his clothes are respectable, and to judge from his face and walk, he's old enough to be Lucentio's father.

LUCENTIO

> And what about him, Tranio?

TRANIO

> If he's an easy mark and buys my story, I think I can get him to pose as Vincentio—and be as ready to vouch for you with Baptista Minola as the real Vincentio would. Go, take your sweetheart and leave him to me.

> LUCENTIO *and* BIANCA *exit.*

> *A* MERCHANT *enters.*

MERCHANT

> May God keep you well, sir.

TRANIO

> *(as* LUCENTIO*)* And you too, sir. Welcome. Are you going far, or is this your destination?

MERCHANT

> This is it, for now. Then, in a week or two, I'll continue on as far as Rome, then on to Tripoli, God willing.

TRANIO
        (*as* LUCENTIO) What countryman, I pray?

MERCHANT
                                              Of Mantua.

TRANIO
80   (*as* LUCENTIO) Of Mantua, sir? Marry, God forbid!
        And come to Padua, careless of your life?

MERCHANT
        My life, sir! how, I pray? For that goes hard.

TRANIO
        'Tis death for anyone in Mantua
        To come to Padua. Know you not the cause?
85   Your ships are stayed at Venice, and the Duke,
        For private quarrel 'twixt your duke and him,
        Hath published and proclaimed it openly.
        'Tis marvel, but that you are but newly come,
        You might have heard it else proclaimed about.

MERCHANT
90   Alas, sir, it is worse for me than so,
        For I have bills for money by exchange
        From Florence, and must here deliver them.

TRANIO
        (*as* LUCENTIO) Well, sir, to do you courtesy,
        This will I do, and this I will advise you.
95   First tell me, have you ever been at Pisa?

MERCHANT
        Ay, sir, in Pisa have I often been,
        Pisa renownèd for grave citizens.

TRANIO
        (*as* LUCENTIO) Among them know you one Vincentio?

MERCHANT
        I know him not, but I have heard of him:
100   A merchant of incomparable wealth.

TRANIO

(*speaking as* LUCENTIO) What country are you from, if I may ask?

MERCHANT

Mantua.

TRANIO

(*as* LUCENTIO) Mantua, sir? Oh Lord, I hope not. And coming to Padua? Do you want to get killed?

MERCHANT

Killed? Why? That would be a little extreme!

TRANIO

It's a capital offense for anyone from Mantua to come to Padua. Didn't you know? The Duke of Padua has publicly proclaimed it. He's feuding with your duke, and all ships from Mantua are being held up at Venice. It's strange that you haven't heard. There are signs up all over town—but I guess it's because you've only just arrived.

MERCHANT

Oh dear, oh dear. This is very bad, very bad. I have promissory notes from Florence that I have to deliver.

TRANIO

(*as* LUCENTIO) Well, look, just to be nice I'll help you out and give you some advice to boot. First tell me, though—have you ever been to Pisa?

MERCHANT

Oh yes, sir, I have often been to Pisa—Pisa, City of Wise Men.

TRANIO

(*as* LUCENTIO) There's one of them called Vincentio? Do you know him?

MERCHANT

I've heard of him but I've never met him. A merchant of unheard-of wealth.

TRANIO

    (as LUCENTIO*)* He is my father, sir, and sooth to say,
    In count'nance somewhat doth resemble you.

BIONDELLO

    (aside) As much as an apple doth an oyster, and all one.

TRANIO

    (as LUCENTIO*)* To save your life in this extremity,
105   This favor will I do you for his sake—
    And think it not the worst of all your fortunes
    That you are like to Sir Vincentio—
    His name and credit shall you undertake,
    And in my house you shall be friendly lodged.
110   Look that you take upon you as you should.
    You understand me, sir. So shall you stay
    Till you have done your business in the city.
    If this be court'sy, sir, accept of it.

MERCHANT

    O sir, I do, and will repute you ever
115   The patron of my life and liberty.

TRANIO

    (as LUCENTIO*)* Then go with me to make the matter good.
    This, by the way, I let you understand:
    My father is here looked for every day
    To pass assurance of a dower in marriage
120   'Twixt me and one Baptista's daughter here.
    In all these circumstances I'll instruct you.
    Go with me to clothe you as becomes you.

Exeunt

TRANIO

(*as* LUCENTIO) He is my father, sir, and I have to tell you—you look a little like him.

BIONDELLO

(*speaking to the audience*) As much as an apple looks like an oyster, but whatever.

TRANIO

(*as* LUCENTIO) Under the circumstance, to save your life, here's what I'm willing to do—and it's actually not an unlucky thing that you happen to look like Sir Vincentio. We'll pass you off as him—you can assume his name and reputation and stay in my house. You just have to act your part, you understand? You'll stay here in the city until you've taken care of your business. If this is kindness, you're welcome to it.

MERCHANT

Oh sir, I accept. And I'll be eternally grateful to you.

TRANIO

(*as* LUCENTIO) Then come with me and we'll set it up. And, by the way, I should probably tell you: my father himself is coming any day to vouch for me in the matter of a dowry—a marriage contract between me and the daughter of a fellow named Baptista. I'll fill you in on the whole situation. Come, let's go and get your costume.

They exit.

ACT 4, SCENE 3

Enter KATHERINE *and* GRUMIO

GRUMIO
　　No, no, forsooth, I dare not for my life.

KATHERINE
　　The more my wrong, the more his spite appears.
　　What, did he marry me to famish me?
　　Beggars that come unto my father's door
5　　Upon entreaty have a present alms.
　　If not, elsewhere they meet with charity.
　　But I, who never knew how to entreat,
　　Nor never needed that I should entreat,
　　Am starved for meat, giddy for lack of sleep,
10　　With oaths kept waking and with brawling fed.
　　And that which spites me more than all these wants,
　　He does it under name of perfect love,
　　As who should say, if I should sleep or eat,
　　'Twere deadly sickness or else present death.
15　　I prithee, go and get me some repast,
　　I care not what, so it be wholesome food.

GRUMIO
　　What say you to a neat's foot?

KATHERINE
　　'Tis passing good. I prithee let me have it.

GRUMIO
　　I fear it is too choleric a meat.
20　　How say you to a fat tripe finely broiled?

KATHERINE
　　I like it well. Good Grumio, fetch it me.

GRUMIO
　　I cannot tell. I fear 'tis choleric. What say you to a piece of
　　beef and mustard?

KATHERINE
　　A dish that I do love to feed upon.

ACT 4, SCENE 3

KATHERINE *and* GRUMIO *enter.*

GRUMIO

No, no, I can't, really. He'd kill me.

KATHERINE

The more I suffer, the more spiteful he becomes. Did he marry me just to starve me? Beggars at my father's door are given money as soon as they ask for it. And if they don't find charity there, they find it someplace else. But I, who have never known how to beg and never had to beg, am starved for food, dizzy with lack of sleep, kept awake with curses and fed with brawling. And what irks me more than all these things put together is that he does it under the pretense of love— as though for me to eat or sleep would bring on fatal illness or sudden death. Please, go and get me something to eat. I don't care what so long as it's nutritious.

GRUMIO

What do you say to a calf's foot?

KATHERINE

Oh, lovely. Can I have some?

GRUMIO

"Choleric" = angry I'm afraid it will raise your blood pressure. What do you say to an ox stomach, nicely broiled?

KATHERINE

I'd love it. Nice Grumio, bring me some.

GRUMIO

I don't know. I'm afraid it will make you too hot, too. What do you say to a piece of beef with mustard?

KATHERINE

A favorite dish of mine.

GRUMIO

25   Ay, but the mustard is too hot a little.

KATHERINE

Why then, the beef, and let the mustard rest.

GRUMIO

Nay then, I will not. You shall have the mustard
Or else you get no beef of Grumio.

KATHERINE

Then both, or one, or anything thou wilt.

GRUMIO

30   Why then, the mustard without the beef.

KATHERINE

Go, get thee gone, thou false deluding slave,

Beats him

That feed'st me with the very name of meat.
Sorrow on thee and all the pack of you
That triumph thus upon my misery.
35   Go, get thee gone, I say.

Enter PETRUCHIO *and* HORTENSIO *with meat*

PETRUCHIO

How fares my Kate? What, sweeting, all amort?

HORTENSIO

Mistress, what cheer?

KATHERINE

                         Faith, as cold as can be.

PETRUCHIO

Pluck up thy spirits. Look cheerfully upon me.
Here love, thou seest how diligent I am,
40   To dress thy meat myself and bring it thee.
I am sure, sweet Kate, this kindness merits thanks.
What, not a word? Nay, then thou lov'st it not
And all my pains is sorted to no proof.
Here, take away this dish.

GRUMIO

Yes, but the mustard is probably too hot.

KATHERINE

Well then, the beef without the mustard.

GRUMIO

Absolutely not. You'll take the mustard or you'll get no beef from Grumio.

KATHERINE

Then both, or one, or anything you like.

GRUMIO

How about the mustard without the beef.

KATHERINE

Get out of here, you measly, lying wretch. *(she beats him.)* You feed me with only the names of foods. To hell with you and the whole pack of you who triumph at my misery. Go on, I said get out of here.

PETRUCHIO *and* HORTENSIO *enter with a dish of meat.*

PETRUCHIO

How is my Kate? Feeling blue, darling?

HORTENSIO

Mistress, how are you?

KATHERINE

Believe me, I've been better.

PETRUCHIO

Cheer up. Give us a smile. Look, love, see how devoted I am? I've prepared a meal for you myself, and here it is. I am sure, sweet Kate, this kindness deserves thanks. What, not a word? I guess you don't want it. Ah well, all my trouble was for nothing. Here, take away the dish.

KATHERINE
                                        I pray you, let it stand.

PETRUCHIO
45   The poorest service is repaid with thanks,
        And so shall mine, before you touch the meat.

KATHERINE
        I thank you, sir.

HORTENSIO
        Signior Petruchio, fie, you are to blame.
        Come, mistress Kate, I'll bear you company.

PETRUCHIO
        (aside to **HORTENSIO***)*
50   Eat it up all, Hortensio, if thou lovest me.—
        Much good do it unto thy gentle heart.
        Kate, eat apace. And now, my honey love,
        Will we return unto thy father's house
        And revel it as bravely as the best,
55   With silken coats and caps and golden rings,
        With ruffs and cuffs and farthingales and things,
        With scarves and fans and double change of brav'ry,
        With amber bracelets, beads, and all this knav'ry.
        What, hast thou dined? The tailor stays thy leisure
60   To deck thy body with his ruffling treasure.

        Enter **TAILOR**

        Come, tailor, let us see these ornaments.
        Lay forth the gown.

        Enter **HABERDASHER**

                                        What news with you, sir?

HABERDASHER
        Here is the cap your Worship did bespeak.

KATHERINE

Please, leave it here.

PETRUCHIO

The smallest service is repaid with thanks. Mine will be, too, before you touch the food.

KATHERINE

Thank you, sir.

HORTENSIO

Shame on you, Petruchio! You are too harsh. Come, mistress Kate, I'll join you.

PETRUCHIO

(speaking so that only HORTENSIO *can hear)* Do me a favor and scarf it all down yourself, Hortensio.—May it do your gentle heart good, Kate. Eat up quickly, my honey lamb, we're off to your father's house to join in the revelry, where we'll dress as well as the best of them, with silk robes and caps and golden rings, collars and cuffs and fancy frocks and things, with scarves and fans and two changes of clothes, amber bracelets, beads, and plenty of gewgaws. All finished? The tailor is waiting to deck you out in ruffled finery.

A TAILOR *enters.*

Now, tailor, let's see what you've got. Lay out the gown.

A HATMAKER *enters.*

What can I do for you, sir?

HATMAKER

Here is the cap your Worship ordered.

PETRUCHIO

    Why, this was molded on a porringer!
65   A velvet dish! Fie, fie, 'tis lewd and filthy!
    Why, 'tis a cockle or a walnut shell,
    A knack, a toy, a trick, a baby's cap.
    Away with it! Come, let me have a bigger.

KATHERINE

    I'll have no bigger. This doth fit the time,
70   And gentlewomen wear such caps as these.

PETRUCHIO

    When you are gentle, you shall have one too,
    And not till then.

HORTENSIO

    (aside) That will not be in haste.

KATHERINE

    Why, sir, I trust I may have leave to speak,
75   And speak I will. I am no child, no babe.
    Your betters have endured me say my mind,
    And if you cannot, best you stop your ears.
    My tongue will tell the anger of my heart
    Or else my heart, concealing it, will break,
80   And, rather than it shall, I will be free
    Even to the uttermost, as I please, in words.

PETRUCHIO

    Why, thou say'st true. It is a paltry cap,
    A custard-coffin, a bauble, a silken pie.
    I love thee well in that thou lik'st it not.

KATHERINE

85   Love me or love me not, I like the cap,
    And it I will have, or I will have none.

Exit HABERDASHER

PETRUCHIO

    Thy gown? Why, ay. Come, tailor, let us see 't.
    O mercy, God! What masking stuff is here?
    What's this? A sleeve? 'Tis like a demi-cannon.

PETRUCHIO

Why, this was modeled on a porridge bowl! It's a velvet dish! No, definitely not! It's cheap and nasty! It's like a cockleshell or a walnut shell, a joke, a prank, a doll's cap. Take it away. Bring me a bigger one.

KATHERINE

I won't have one any bigger. This is the fashion. Gentlewomen are wearing caps like this right now.

PETRUCHIO

When you are gentle, you shall have one, too, and not till then.

HORTENSIO

(to himself) That won't be anytime soon.

KATHERINE

Sir, I think I have the right to speak, and speak I certainly will. I am not a child or an infant. Better men than you have heard me speak my mind, and if you can't take it, then you'd better plug your ears. I'll express my anger or die concealing it. And rather than have that happen, I'll give myself permission to speak as freely as I like, whatever I may have to say.

PETRUCHIO

You know, you're right. It's a measly little cap, a dessert crust, a plaything, a silk pie. I love you all the more for not liking it.

KATHERINE

I don't care if you love me or not, I like the cap and I'll have it or I won't have any.

HATMAKER exits.

PETRUCHIO

Now, your gown? Yes, yes. Come, tailor, show it to us. Merciful God! What sort of costume do we have here? What do you call this? A sleeve? It's like a cannon.

90   What, up and down, carved like an apple tart?
        Here's snip and nip and cut and slish and slash,
        Like to a censer in a barber's shop.
        Why, what i' devil's name, tailor, call'st thou this?

HORTENSIO
        (aside) I see she's like to have neither cap nor gown.

TAILOR
95   You bid me make it orderly and well,
        According to the fashion and the time.

PETRUCHIO
        Marry, and did. But if you be remembered,
        I did not bid you mar it to the time.
        Go, hop me over every kennel home,
100   For you shall hop without my custom, sir.
        I'll none of it. Hence, make your best of it.

KATHERINE
        I never saw a better-fashioned gown,
        More quaint, more pleasing, nor more commendable.
        Belike you mean to make a puppet of me.

PETRUCHIO
105   Why, true, he means to make a puppet of thee.

TAILOR
        She says your Worship means to make a puppet of her.

PETRUCHIO
        O monstrous arrogance! Thou liest, thou thread, thou
        thimble,
        Thou yard, three-quarters, half-yard, quarter, nail!
110   Thou flea, thou nit, thou winter cricket thou!
        Braved in mine own house with a skein of thread?
        Away, thou rag, thou quantity, thou remnant,
        Or I shall so be-mete thee with thy yard
        As thou shalt think on prating whilst thou liv'st!
115   I tell thee, I, that thou hast marred her gown.

What have you done? Carved it up and down like an apple tart? Snip and snip and cut and slash—it's got more holes than a sieve! What in the world do you call this, tailor!

HORTENSIO

(to himself) I see she's likely to have neither cap nor gown.

TAILOR

You told me to make it well and properly and in keeping with the current style.

PETRUCHIO

Certainly, I did. But if you remember, I didn't tell you to parody the style. Go on home, sir. You've lost me as a customer. I won't take it. Do whatever you want with it.

KATHERINE

I never saw a better-designed gown, more elegant and pleasing and well made. Perhaps you think you can make me into some sort of plaything?

PETRUCHIO

Yes, that's it! The tailor thinks he can make you into some sort of plaything.

TAILOR

She says your Worship thinks *you* can make her into some sort of plaything.

PETRUCHIO

What monstrous arrogance! It's a lie, you thread, you thimble, you measurement! You flea, you louse, you winter cricket! Disrespected in my own house by a spool of thread! Get out of here you rag, you remnant, you piece of yardage, or I'll measure you within an inch of your life with your own yardstick, and you'll remember your yammering for the rest of your life. I tell you, you've ruined her gown.

TAILOR
Your Worship is deceived. The gown is made
Just as my master had direction.
Grumio gave order how it should be done.

GRUMIO
I gave him no order. I gave him the stuff.

TAILOR
120 But how did you desire it should be made?

GRUMIO
Marry, sir, with needle and thread.

TAILOR
But did you not request to have it cut?

GRUMIO
Thou hast faced many things.

TAILOR
I have.

GRUMIO
125 Face not me. Thou hast braved many men; brave not me. I
will neither be faced nor braved. I say unto thee, I bid thy
master cut out the gown, but I did not bid him cut it to
pieces. *Ergo,* thou liest.

TAILOR
Why, here is the note of the fashion to testify.

Holds up a paper

PETRUCHIO
130 Read it.

GRUMIO
The note lies in 's throat, if he say I said so.

TAILOR
(reads) "*Imprimis,* a loose-bodied gown—"

TAILOR

It's not true. The gown was made just as my master was directed. Grumio gave the order for how it should be done.

GRUMIO

I gave him no order. I gave him the material.

TAILOR

But how did you want it made?

GRUMIO

With a needle and thread.

TAILOR

But didn't you expect us to cut the cloth?

GRUMIO

To face means to decorate with trim.

You've faced many things, haven't you?

TAILOR

I have.

GRUMIO

Well, don't face off with me. You have bested many things, well don't try and best me. I will not be faced or bested. I tell you I requested that your master cut out the gown, but I didn't ask him to cut it all to pieces. Therefore, it follows you're a liar.

TAILOR

Why, here is the order to prove it.

He holds up a piece of paper.

PETRUCHIO

Read it.

GRUMIO

The note is a big fat liar if it says I said so.

TAILOR

(reading) "Item one, a loose-bodied gown—"

GRUMIO
Master, if ever I said "loose-bodied gown," sew me in the
skirts of it, and beat me to death with a bottom of brown
135 thread. I said "a gown."

PETRUCHIO
Proceed.

TAILOR
(reads) "With a small-compassed cape—"

GRUMIO
I confess the cape.

TAILOR
(reads) "With a trunk sleeve—"

GRUMIO
140 I confess two sleeves.

TAILOR
(reads) "The sleeves curiously cut."

PETRUCHIO
Ay, there's the villany.

GRUMIO
Error i' the bill, sir, error i' the bill! I commanded the
sleeves should be cut out and sewed up again, and that I'll
145 prove upon thee, though thy little finger be armed in a
thimble.

TAILOR
This is true that I say: an I had thee in place where, thou
shouldst know it.

GRUMIO
I am for thee straight. Take thou the bill, give me thy mete-
150 yard, and spare not me.

HORTENSIO
God-a-mercy, Grumio! Then he shall have no odds.

PETRUCHIO
Well, sir, in brief, the gown is not for me.

GRUMIO
You are i' the right, sir, 'tis for my mistress.

GRUMIO

Grumio acts as if "loose-bodied" meant "intended for a loose woman."

Master, if ever I said "loose-bodied gown," sew me into the skirts of it and beat me to death with a bobbin of brown thread. I said "a gown."

PETRUCHIO

Go on.

TAILOR

(he reads) "With a half-circle cape—"

GRUMIO

I admit the cape.

TAILOR

(he reads) "With a wide sleeve—"

GRUMIO

I admit two sleeves.

TAILOR

(he reads) "The sleeves carefully cut."

PETRUCHIO

Ah, there's the problem.

GRUMIO

Error in the bill, sir, error in the bill! I ordered that the sleeves be cut out and sewed up again, and I'll prove it in combat even if your little finger is armed with your thimble.

TAILOR

What I say is true. And if this were a fitting place, I'd prove it.

GRUMIO

I am ready for you. You take the bill and I'll take your yardstick. Do your worst!

HORTENSIO

God have mercy, Grumio! He won't have a chance.

PETRUCHIO

Well, sir, the gown is not for me.

GRUMIO

You are right, it's for my mistress.

PETRUCHIO
Go, take it up unto thy master's use.

GRUMIO
155   Villain, not for thy life! Take up my mistress' gown for thy
master's use!

PETRUCHIO
Why, sir, what's your conceit in that?

GRUMIO
O, sir, the conceit is deeper than you think for. Take up my
mistress' gown to his master's use! O, fie, fie, fie!

PETRUCHIO
160   *(aside)* Hortensio, say thou wilt see the tailor paid.
(to TAILOR*)* Go, take it hence. Begone, and say no more.

HORTENSIO
(aside to TAILOR*)*
Tailor, I'll pay thee for thy gown tomorrow.
Take no unkindness of his hasty words.
Away, I say. Commend me to thy master.

Exit TAILOR

PETRUCHIO
165   Well, come, my Kate. We will unto your father's
Even in these honest mean habiliments.
Our purses shall be proud, our garments poor,
For 'tis the mind that makes the body rich,
And as the sun breaks through the darkest clouds,
170   So honor peereth in the meanest habit.
What, is the jay more precious than the lark
Because his feathers are more beautiful?
Or is the adder better than the eel
Because his painted skin contents the eye?

NO FEAR SHAKESPEARE

PETRUCHIO

Go, take it away and let your master make whatever use of it he can.

GRUMIO

Certainly not! Take off my mistress' gown for your master's use!

PETRUCHIO

Why, what's the problem?

GRUMIO

Oh, sir, the problem goes far deeper than you realize. Take up my mistress' gown for his master's use! Oh, that's disgusting!

PETRUCHIO

(speaking so that only HORTENSIO *can hear)* Hortensio, tell the tailor you'll make sure he gets paid. *(to* TAILOR*)* Take it away. Off you go. There's no more to be said.

HORTENSIO

(speaking so that only TAILOR *can hear)* Tailor, I'll pay you for the gown tomorrow. Don't be offended at his angry words. Go on, then. Regards to your master.

> TAILOR *exits.*

PETRUCHIO

Ah well, my Kate. We'll go to your father's house dressed as we are, in simple but honest clothes. Our purses shall be rich, our garments poor. After all, it's the mind that enriches the body, and just as the sun shines through the darkest clouds, well, that's how clearly honor peeps through even the humblest style of dress. I mean, is the jay more precious than the lark because his feather is more beautiful? Is the snake better than the eel because the pattern on his back pleases the eye?

175   Oh, no, good Kate. Neither art thou the worse
    For this poor furniture and mean array.
    If thou account'st it shame, lay it on me,
    And therefore frolic! We will hence forthwith
    To feast and sport us at thy father's house.
180   *(to* GRUMIO*)* Go, call my men, and let us straight to him,
    And bring our horses unto Long Lane end.
    There will we mount, and thither walk on foot.
    Let's see, I think 'tis now some seven o'clock,
    And well we may come there by dinnertime.

KATHERINE
185   I dare assure you, sir, 'tis almost two,
    And 'twill be supper time ere you come there.

PETRUCHIO
    It shall be seven ere I go to horse.
    Look what I speak, or do, or think to do,
    You are still crossing it. Sirs, let 't alone.
190   I will not go today, and ere I do
    It shall be what o'clock I say it is.

HORTENSIO
    (aside) Why, so this gallant will command the sun.

Exeunt

Hardly, Kate. By the same token you are worth no less for your simple clothes and lack of finery. If you regard it as shameful, put the shame on me. So, let's perk up! We're off to eat and whoop it up at your father's house.*(to* GRUMIO*)* Go, call my men so we can leave right away. And bring our horses to the end of Long Lane. We'll walk there on foot and mount up there. Let's see, I think it must be seven o'clock, so we should get there easily by lunchtime.

KATHERINE

I hate to say it, but it's almost two and we won't get there before suppertime.

PETRUCHIO

It shall be seven o'clock before I get on my horse. Whatever I say, or think, or do, you're continually contradicting it. Sirs, never mind. We won't go today—or any day until it's clear that it shall be whatever time I say it is.

HORTENSIO

(to himself) I see this fellow intends to command the sun.

They all exit.

ACT 4, SCENE 4

Enter TRANIO *as* LUCENTIO *and the* MERCHANT *booted and dressed like* VINCENTIO

TRANIO
(*as* LUCENTIO) Sir, this is the house. Please it you that I call?

MERCHANT
Ay, what else? and but I be deceived,
Signior Baptista may remember me,
Near twenty years ago, in Genoa,
5   Where we were lodgers at the Pegasus.

TRANIO
(*as* LUCENTIO) 'Tis well; and hold your own, in any case,
With such austerity as 'longeth to a father.

MERCHANT
I warrant you.

Enter BIONDELLO

But, sir, here comes your boy.
'Twere good he were schooled.

TRANIO
10   (*as* LUCENTIO) Fear you not him.—Sirrah Biondello,
Now do your duty throughly, I advise you.
Imagine 'twere the right Vincentio.

BIONDELLO
Tut, fear not me.

TRANIO
(*as* LUCENTIO) But hast thou done thy errand to Baptista?

BIONDELLO
15   I told him that your father was at Venice,
And that you looked for him this day in Padua.

ACT 4, SCENE 4

TRANIO *enters, disguised as* LUCENTIO, *with the* MERCHANT, *dressed like* VINCENTIO

TRANIO

(as LUCENTIO*)* Sir, this is the house. Would you like me to ring?

MERCHANT

Yes, certainly. Unless I am mistaken, Signior Baptista may remember me from the Pegasus in Genoa, where we both stayed twenty years ago.

TRANIO

(as LUCENTIO*)* Fine, fine. Just play your part and act as serious as a father should.

MERCHANT

Of course I will.

BIONDELLO *enters.*

But, sir, here comes your servant. Better fill him in.

TRANIO

(as LUCENTIO*)* Don't worry about him.—You there, Biondello, now act your part convincingly. Behave as though this were the real Vincentio.

BIONDELLO

Don't worry about me.

TRANIO

(as LUCENTIO*)* And did you take the message to Baptista?

BIONDELLO

I told him that your father was in Venice, and that you expected him to arrive in Padua today.

TRANIO
(as LUCENTIO*)* Thou'rt a tall fellow. Hold thee that to drink.

Gives money

Enter BAPTISTA *and* LUCENTIO

Here comes Baptista. Set your countenance, sir.

MERCHANT *takes off his cap*

Signior Baptista, you are happily met.—
20   Sir, this is the gentleman I told you of.
I pray you stand good father to me now.
Give me Bianca for my patrimony.

MERCHANT
(as VINCENTIO*)* Soft son.—
Sir, by your leave, having come to Padua
25   To gather in some debts, my son Lucentio
Made me acquainted with a weighty cause
Of love between your daughter and himself.
And, for the good report I hear of you
And for the love he beareth to your daughter
30   And she to him, to stay him not too long,
I am content, in a good father's care,
To have him matched. And if you please to like
No worse than I, upon some agreement
Me shall you find ready and willing
35   With one consent to have her so bestowed,
For curious I cannot be with you,
Signior Baptista, of whom I hear so well.

BAPTISTA
Sir, pardon me in what I have to say.
Your plainness and your shortness please me well.
40   Right true it is your son Lucentio here
Doth love my daughter and she loveth him,
Or both dissemble deeply their affections.

TRANIO

> (*as* LUCENTIO) Good lad! Here, buy yourself a drink on me.

He gives BIONDELLO *some money.*

BAPTISTA *and* LUCENTIO *enter.*

> Here comes Baptista. Places, everyone!

MERCHANT *takes off his cap.*

> Signior Baptista, I'm glad to see you.—Sir, this is the gentleman I told you of. I hope you'll be a good father to me now. Give me Bianca for my inheritance.

MERCHANT

> (*as* VINCENTIO) Hush, son.—Sir, may I? Having come to Padua to collect some debts, my son Lucentio acquainted me with a serious matter, namely the love between your daughter and himself. Now, since I've heard good reports of you, and in view of the love between your daughter and my son, I'm willing to give my consent to his marriage right away. So, if you think you can put up with no worse a man than I am, you'll find me willing, pending some agreement, to see your daughter betrothed to him. I can't haggle with you, Signior Baptista. I have too much respect for you.

BAPTISTA

> Sir, pardon me for what I am about to say. I appreciate your frankness and your brevity. It's true that your son Lucentio here loves my daughter, and she loves him—or else they're putting on quite an act.

And therefore, if you say no more than this,
That like a father you will deal with him
45   And pass my daughter a sufficient dower,
The match is made, and all is done.
Your son shall have my daughter with consent.

TRANIO
      (as LUCENTIO*)*
      I thank you, sir. Where then do you know best
      We be affied and such assurance ta'en
50   As shall with either part's agreement stand?

BAPTISTA
      Not in my house, Lucentio, for you know
      Pitchers have ears, and I have many servants.
      Besides, old Gremio is heark'ning still,
      And happily we might be interrupted.

TRANIO
55   *(as* LUCENTIO*)* Then at my lodging, an it like you.
      There doth my father lie, and there this night
      We'll pass the business privately and well.
      Send for your daughter by your servant here.
      My boy shall fetch the scrivener presently.
60   The worst is this, that at so slender warning
      You are like to have a thin and slender pittance.

BAPTISTA
      It likes me well.—Cambio, hie you home,
      And bid Bianca make her ready straight.
      And, if you will, tell what hath happenèd:
65   Lucentio's father is arrived in Padua,
      And how she's like to be Lucentio's wife.

                                          Exit LUCENTIO

BIONDELLO
      I pray the gods she may, with all my heart!

Therefore, provided that you assure me that you will treat your son as a father should and offer my daughter a sufficient dowry, we'll call it a match and be done with it. Your son will have my consent to marry my daughter.

TRANIO

(*as* LUCENTIO) Thank you, sir. Where can we draw up the necessary papers and get this settled?

BAPTISTA

Not in my house, Lucentio. My servants might overhear, and old Gremio is still hanging around, so we might be interrupted.

TRANIO

(*as* LUCENTIO) Then at my place, if you like. That's where my father's staying. We can get everything sorted out in private there tonight. Send your servant for Bianca. Mine shall go and fetch the notary. The only drawback is that, with such short notice, we'll be able to offer you only modest refreshment.

BAPTISTA

This is all very acceptable.—Cambio, hurry home and tell Bianca to get ready right away and, if you don't mind, tell her what's happened: that Lucentio's father has arrived in Padua, and that she's likely to become Lucentio's wife.

LUCENTIO *exits.*

BIONDELLO

I hope with all my heart she will!

TRANIO
(as LUCENTIO) Dally not with the gods, but get thee gone.—
Signior Baptista, shall I lead the way?

70 Welcome! One mess is like to be your cheer.
Come, sir, we will better it in Pisa.

BAPTISTA
I follow you.

Exeunt TRANIO, MERCHANT, *and* BAPTISTA

BIONDELLO
Cambio.

LUCENTIO
What sayest thou, Biondello?

BIONDELLO
75 You saw my master wink and laugh upon you?

LUCENTIO
Biondello, what of that?

BIONDELLO
Faith, nothing; but 'has left me here behind to expound the
meaning or moral of his signs and tokens.

LUCENTIO
I pray thee, moralize them.

BIONDELLO
80 Then thus: Baptista is safe, talking with the deceiving
father of a deceitful son.

LUCENTIO
And what of him?

BIONDELLO
His daughter is to be brought by you to the supper.

LUCENTIO
And then?

BIONDELLO
85 The old priest at Saint Luke's Church is at your command
at all hours.

LUCENTIO
And what of all this?

TRANIO

(*as* LUCENTIO) Forget about your heart and get busy.— Signior Baptista, shall I lead the way? You'll be welcome, though dinner will probably be only one course. We'll make it up to you in Pisa.

BAPTISTA

I'll come with you.

TRANIO, MERCHANT, *and* BAPTISTA *exit.*

BIONDELLO

Cambio.

LUCENTIO

What is it, Biondello?

BIONDELLO

You saw my master wink and laugh at you?

LUCENTIO

What about it?

BIONDELLO

Nothing. It's just that he left me here behind to interpret his signs and signals.

LUCENTIO

Please, educate me.

BIONDELLO

Here's the deal: we're safe on the Baptista front. He's talking with the bogus father about the bogus son.

LUCENTIO

And so—?

BIONDELLO

You are to bring his daughter to the supper.

LUCENTIO

And then?

BIONDELLO

The old priest at Saint Luke's Church is at your command at all hours.

LUCENTIO

And what of all this?

BIONDELLO

I cannot tell, except they are busied about a counterfeit
assurance. Take you assurance of her cum privilegio ad
90   imprimendum solum. To th' church take the priest, clerk,
and some sufficient honest witnesses.
If this be not that you look for, I have no more to say,
But bid Bianca farewell forever and a day.

LUCENTIO

Hear'st thou, Biondello?

BIONDELLO

95   I cannot tarry. I knew a wench married in an afternoon as
she went to the garden for parsley to stuff a rabbit, and so
may you, sir. And so adieu, sir. My master hath appointed
me to go to Saint Luke's to bid the priest be ready to come
against you come with your appendix.

Exit

LUCENTIO

100   I may, and will, if she be so contented.
She will be pleased. Then wherefore should I doubt?
Hap what hap may, I'll roundly go about her.
It shall go hard if "Cambio" go without her.

Exit

BIONDELLO

> I don't know, except they are busy with some phony guarantee. So go and put your stamp on the girl. Go to the church: take the priest, the clerk, and some reasonably honest witnesses. If this isn't what you've been hoping for, I have no more to say except that you ought to say goodbye to Bianca forever.

LUCENTIO

> Listen, Biondello—

BIONDELLO

> I can't stay. I knew a girl who was married in an afternoon as she went to the garden for parsley to stuff a rabbit. It could happen to you. Farewell, sir. My master has instructed me to go to Saint Luke's to tell the priest to be ready in case you should show up with your better half.

He exits.

LUCENTIO

> I may. I will if she likes the idea. She will be pleased. Then why am I worried? Oh well, whatever. I'll ask her straight out. It will be hard if "Cambio" loses her.

He exits.

ACT 4, SCENE 5

Enter PETRUCHIO, KATHERINE, HORTENSIO, *and Servants*

PETRUCHIO
Come on, i' God's name, once more toward our father's.
Good Lord, how bright and goodly shines the moon!

KATHERINE
The moon? The sun! It is not moonlight now.

PETRUCHIO
I say it is the moon that shines so bright.

KATHERINE
5   I know it is the sun that shines so bright.

PETRUCHIO
Now, by my mother's son, and that's myself,
It shall be moon, or star, or what I list,
Or e'er I journey to your father's house.
(to servants) Go on, and fetch our horses back again.—
10   Evermore crossed and crossed, nothing but crossed!

HORTENSIO
(to KATHERINE*)* Say as he says, or we shall never go.

KATHERINE
Forward, I pray, since we have come so far,
And be it moon, or sun, or what you please.
An if you please to call it a rush candle,
15   Henceforth I vow it shall be so for me.

PETRUCHIO
I say it is the moon.

KATHERINE
I know it is the moon.

PETRUCHIO
Nay, then you lie. It is the blessèd sun.

ACT 4, SCENE 5

PETRUCHIO, KATHERINE, *and* HORTENSIO *enter, accompanied by servants.*

PETRUCHIO

Come, let's continue on toward your father's house. Good Lord, how bright and splendid is the moon tonight!

KATHERINE

The moon? You mean the sun! It is not nighttime now.

PETRUCHIO

I say it's the moon that shines so bright.

KATHERINE

I know it's the sun that shines so bright.

PETRUCHIO

Now, by my mother's son, and that's me, it will be moon or star or whatever I want before I'll travel to your father's house. *(to servants)* Go return our horses.— Constantly contradicted and contradicted, and nothing but contradicted!

HORTENSIO

(to KATHERINE*)* Say what he wants or we'll never go.

KATHERINE

Since we've come this far, please—let's continue on. And whatever it is—moon or sun or anything you like—if you want to call it a tea candle, that's what it is as far as I'm concerned. From now on, I promise.

PETRUCHIO

I say it's the moon.

KATHERINE

I know it's the moon.

PETRUCHIO

Well, you're a liar, then. It's the blessed sun.

KATHERINE
>Then God be blessed, it is the blessèd sun.
>20 But sun it is not, when you say it is not,
>And the moon changes even as your mind.
>What you will have it named, even that it is,
>And so it shall be so for Katherine.

HORTENSIO
>Petruchio, go thy ways; the field is won.

PETRUCHIO
>25 Well, forward, forward! Thus the bowl should run,
>And not unluckily against the bias.
>But, soft! Company is coming here.

Enter VINCENTIO

(to VINCENTIO*)*
>Good morrow, gentle mistress, where away?—
>Tell me, sweet Kate, and tell me truly too,
>30 Hast thou beheld a fresher gentlewoman?
>Such war of white and red within her cheeks!
>What stars do spangle heaven with such beauty
>As those two eyes become that heavenly face?—
>Fair lovely maid, once more good day to thee.—
>35 Sweet Kate, embrace her for her beauty's sake.

HORTENSIO
>*(aside)* He will make the man mad, to make a woman of him.

KATHERINE
>Young budding virgin, fair and fresh and sweet,
>Whither away, or where is thy abode?
>Happy the parents of so fair a child.
>40 Happier the man whom favorable stars
>Allot thee for his lovely bedfellow!

KATHERINE

> Then God be praised, it *is* the blessed sun. But it is not the sun when you say it is not, and the moon changes according to your mind. Whatever you want to call a thing, that's what it is—and that's what it will always be for me.

HORTENSIO

> Petruchio, do whatever you like. You've won.

PETRUCHIO

> Well, onward, then. That's how things should be—straight and smooth. But, hang on! I hear someone coming.

> VINCENTIO *enters.*

> *(to* VINCENTIO*)* Good morning, young miss, where are you going?—Tell me, sweet Kate, and tell me truly, have you ever seen a young gentlewoman blooming more with health? The way the shades of white and red compete in her complexion. Which of the stars in heaven shine with such beauty as the two eyes that sparkle in that heavenly face? Fair lovely maid, once more good day to you.—Sweet Kate, embrace her for her beauty.

HORTENSIO

> *(speaking so that only the audience can hear)* He will drive the man mad pretending he thinks he's a woman.

KATHERINE

> Young budding virgin, fair and pure and sweet, where are you off to? Or where do you live? Your parents are lucky to have such a lovely child. And luckier still is the man who gets to be your husband and share your bed.

PETRUCHIO
Why, how now, Kate! I hope thou art not mad.
This is a man—old, wrinkled, faded, withered—
And not a maiden, as thou say'st he is.

KATHERINE
45 Pardon, old father, my mistaking eyes
That have been so bedazzled with the sun
That everything I look on seemeth green.
Now I perceive thou art a reverend father.
Pardon, I pray thee, for my mad mistaking.

PETRUCHIO
50 Do, good old grandsire, and withal make known
Which way thou travellest. If along with us,
We shall be joyful of thy company.

VINCENTIO
Fair sir, and you, my merry mistress,
That with your strange encounter much amazed me,
55 My name is called Vincentio, my dwelling Pisa,
And bound I am to Padua, there to visit
A son of mine which long I have not seen.

PETRUCHIO
What is his name?

VINCENTIO
Lucentio, gentle sir.

PETRUCHIO
60 Happily met, the happier for thy son.
And now by law as well as reverend age,
I may entitle thee my loving father.
The sister to my wife, this gentlewoman,
Thy son by this hath married. Wonder not
65 Nor be grieved. She is of good esteem,
Her dowry wealthy, and of worthy birth.
Beside, so qualified as may beseem
The spouse of any noble gentleman.

PETRUCHIO

> Why, dear me, Kate! I hope you haven't lost your mind. This is not a maiden, as you say, but an old man—wrinkled, faded, and withered.

KATHERINE

> Sir, pardon my imperfect eyes, which have been so blinded by the sun that everything I look at appears green. Now I can see that you're an elderly gentleman. Do forgive me for my crazy error.

"Green" here means "young."

PETRUCHIO

> Do, good old grandfather, and while you're at it, tell us which way you're traveling. If we're all headed in the same direction, we'd love your company.

VINCENTIO

> Well, sir, and you, witty lady, who gave me quite a turn with your strange talk, my name is Vincentio, my hometown Pisa, and I am traveling to Padua to visit a son of mine whom I haven't seen in a long while.

PETRUCHIO

> What is his name?

VINCENTIO

> Lucentio, sir.

PETRUCHIO

> A fortunate coincidence—more fortunate for your son. I can now call you "father" in a legal sense, not just out of respect for your age. The sister of my wife, this lady here, is married to your son. And there's no need for wonder or worry. His bride is well thought of, with a rich dowry and noble birth—a fit wife for any nobleman.

Let me embrace with old Vincentio,
70   And wander we to see thy honest son,
Who will of thy arrival be full joyous.

VINCENTIO
But is this true, or is it else your pleasure,
Like pleasant travelers, to break a jest
Upon the company you overtake?

HORTENSIO
75   I do assure thee, father, so it is.

PETRUCHIO
Come, go along and see the truth hereof,
For our first merriment hath made thee jealous.

Exeunt all but HORTENSIO

HORTENSIO
Well, Petruchio, this has put me in heart.
Have to my widow, and if she be froward,
80   Then hast thou taught Hortensio to be untoward.

Exit

Let me embrace the father of Lucentio, and then we'll journey on to see your son, who will rejoice at your arrival.

VINCENTIO

Is all this true? Or is this your way of livening up your travels—playing jokes on people you meet on the way?

HORTENSIO

I assure you, sir, it's true.

PETRUCHIO

Look, come along with us and see the truth for yourself. Our earlier joke has made you understandably suspicious.

Everyone but HORTENSIO *exits.*

HORTENSIO

Well, Petruchio, all this is very encouraging. I'll visit my widow now, and if she proves difficult to manage, I'll know how to make myself impossible.

He exits.

ACT FIVE

SCENE 1

Enter BIONDELLO, LUCENTIO, *and* BIANCA. GREMIO *is out before*

BIONDELLO
Softly and swiftly, sir, for the priest is ready.

LUCENTIO
I fly, Biondello. But they may chance to need thee at home.
Therefore leave us.

Exit LUCENTIO *with* BIANCA

BIONDELLO
Nay, faith, I'll see the church a' your back, and then come
5   back to my master's as soon as I can.

Exit

GREMIO
I marvel Cambio comes not all this while.

Enter PETRUCHIO, KATHERINE, VINCENTIO,
and GRUMIO, *with Attendants*

PETRUCHIO
Sir, here's the door. This is Lucentio's house.
My father's bears more toward the marketplace.
Thither must I, and here I leave you, sir.

VINCENTIO
10   You shall not choose but drink before you go.
I think I shall command your welcome here,
And, by all likelihood, some cheer is toward.

Knocks

ACT FIVE
SCENE 1

BIONDELLO, LUCENTIO, *and* BIANCA *enter.* GREMIO *is already onstage.*

BIONDELLO

Quickly and quietly, sir. The priest is already there.

LUCENTIO

We're off, Biondello. But they may need you at home, so you go on back.

LUCENTIO *and* BIANCA *exit.*

BIONDELLO

I'll see them safely married first and then hurry back to my master's.

He exits.

GREMIO

I wonder why Cambio hasn't shown up in all this time.

PETRUCHIO, KATHERINE, VINCENTIO, *and* GRUMIO *enter, with attendants.*

PETRUCHIO

Here is the door, sir. This is Lucentio's house. My father-in-law lives closer to the marketplace. That's where I'm going now, so I'll leave you here.

VINCENTIO

You must not go without having a drink first. I think I may presume to welcome you, and they're probably preparing some kind of feast to welcome me.

He knocks.

GREMIO
> They're busy within. You were best knock louder.

MERCHANT *looks out of the window*

MERCHANT
> *(as* VINCENTIO*)* What's he that knocks as he would beat
15 down the gate?

VINCENTIO
> Is Signior Lucentio within, sir?

MERCHANT
> *(as* VINCENTIO*)* He's within, sir, but not to be spoken withal.

VINCENTIO
> What if a man bring him a hundred pound or two to make
> merry withal?

MERCHANT
20 > *(as* VINCENTIO*)* Keep your hundred pounds to yourself. He
> shall need none so long as I live.

PETRUCHIO
> *(to* VINCENTIO*)* Nay, I told you your son was well beloved in
> Padua.—Do you hear, sir? To leave frivolous
> circumstances, I pray you tell Signior Lucentio that his
25 > father is come from Pisa and is here at the door to speak with
> him.

MERCHANT
> *(as* VINCENTIO*)* Thou liest. His father is come from Padua
> and here looking out at the window.

VINCENTIO
> Art thou his father?

MERCHANT
30 > *(as* VINCENTIO*)* Ay, sir, so his mother says, if I may believe
> her.

GREMIO

They're pretty busy in there. You'd better knock louder.

The MERCHANT *looks out the window.*

MERCHANT

(as VINCENTIO*)* Who's that breaking down the door?

VINCENTIO

Is Signior Lucentio at home, sir?

MERCHANT

(as VINCENTIO*)* Yes, he's at home, but he can't be disturbed.

VINCENTIO

What if a fellow were bringing him a couple of hundred pounds to toss around?

MERCHANT

(as VINCENTIO*)* Keep your hundreds. He won't need them as long as I'm living.

PETRUCHIO

(to VINCENTIO*)* I told you your son was popular in Padua. Hear that, sir? *(to* MERCHANT*)* Games aside, though, would you be good enough to tell Signior Lucentio that his father has arrived from Pisa and stands at the door waiting to speak with him?

MERCHANT

(as VINCENTIO*)* You lie. His father is already in Padua. In fact, he's standing right here looking out the window.

VINCENTIO

You're his father?

MERCHANT

(as VINCENTIO*)* Yes, sir—according to his mother, if I can believe her.

PETRUCHIO
   (to VINCENTIO*)* Why, how now, gentleman! Why, this is flat
   knavery to take upon you another man's name.

MERCHANT
   (as VINCENTIO*)* Lay hands on the villain. I believe he means
35   to cozen somebody in this city under my countenance.

Enter BIONDELLO

BIONDELLO
   (aside) I have seen them in the church together. God send
   'em good shipping! But who is here? Mine old master
   Vincentio! Now we are undone and brought to nothing.

VINCENTIO
   (to BIONDELLO*)* Come hither, crack-hemp.

BIONDELLO
40   Hope I may choose, sir.

VINCENTIO
   Come hither, you rogue! What, have you forgot me?

BIONDELLO
   Forgot you! No, sir. I could not forget you, for I never saw
   you before in all my life.

VINCENTIO
   What, you notorious villain, didst thou never see thy
45   master's father, Vincentio?

BIONDELLO
   What, my old worshipful old master? Yes, marry, sir. See
   where he looks out of the window.

VINCENTIO
   Is 't so, indeed.

Beats BIONDELLO

BIONDELLO
   Help, help, help! Here's a madman will murder me.

NO FEAR SHAKESPEARE

PETRUCHIO

> *(to* VINCENTIO*)* What? Why this is out and out robbery! To appropriate another man's name.

MERCHANT

> *(as* VINCENTIO*)* Arrest the wretch. I think he means to bamboozle someone in this city while pretending to be me.

> BIONDELLO *enters.*

BIONDELLO

> *(to himself)* Well, I've seen them married. Good luck to them! Uh-oh. What's this? It's my master's father, Vincentio! Now we're in trouble. Everything's ruined.

VINCENTIO

> *(to* BIONDELLO*)* Come here, you scoundrel.

BIONDELLO

> I believe I have some choice in the matter, sir.

VINCENTIO

> Come here, you wretch! What, have you forgotten me?

BIONDELLO

> Forgotten you! No, sir. I could not forget you, since I never saw you before in my life.

VINCENTIO

> Despicable brute! Never seen your master's father, Vincentio?

BIONDELLO

> My honorable, reverend master? Yes, of course. There he is at the window.

VINCENTIO

> Is that so?

> *He beats* BIONDELLO.

BIONDELLO

> Help, help, help! This madman will murder me.

Exit

MERCHANT

50   *(as* VINCENTIO*)* Help, son! Help, Signior Baptista!

Exit from above

PETRUCHIO

Prithee, Kate, let's stand aside and see the end of this
controversy.

They retire

Enter MERCHANT *below,* TRANIO, BAPTISTA, *and Servants*

TRANIO

(as LUCENTIO*)* Sir, what are you that offer to beat my
servant?

VINCENTIO

55   What am I, sir! Nay, what are you, sir? O immortal gods! O
fine villain! A silken doublet, a velvet hose, a scarlet cloak,
and a copatain hat! Oh, I am undone, I am undone! While
I play the good husband at home, my son and my servant
spend all at the university.

TRANIO

60   *(as* LUCENTIO*)* How now, what's the matter?

BAPTISTA

What, is the man lunatic?

TRANIO

(as LUCENTIO*)* Sir, you seem a sober ancient gentleman by
your habit, but your words show you a madman. Why, sir,
what 'cerns it you if I wear pearl and gold? I thank my good
65   father I am able to maintain it.

VINCENTIO

Thy father! O villain! He is a sailmaker in Bergamo.

He exits.

MERCHANT

(*as* VINCENTIO) Help, son! Help, Signior Baptista!

He exits from above.

PETRUCHIO

What do you think, Kate, shall we hang back and see how this conflict finishes?

They draw back.

The MERCHANT *enters below with* TRANIO *as* LUCENTIO, BAPTISTA, *and servants.*

TRANIO

(*as* LUCENTIO) How dare you beat my servant, sir?

VINCENTIO

How dare I? How dare *you,* sir? Oh, cruel gods! Oh, clever villain! A silk doublet, velvet hose, a scarlet cloak, and a high-brimmed hat! Oh, I am destroyed, I am destroyed! While I sat counting my pennies at home, my son and my servant have squandered all my money at the university.

TRANIO

(*as* LUCENTIO) Heavens, what's the matter?

BAPTISTA

What, is the man crazy?

TRANIO

(*as* LUCENTIO) Sir, you seem from your clothes to be a sober, respectable old gentleman, but your words show you to be a madman. What do you care if I wear pearls and gold? Thanks to my father, I can afford to.

VINCENTIO

Your father! Why, you scoundrel! Your father is a sail-maker in Bergamo.

BAPTISTA
> You mistake, sir, you mistake, sir. Pray, what do you think
> is his name?

VINCENTIO
> His name! As if I knew not his name! I have brought him up
70 > ever since he was three years old, and his name is Tranio.

MERCHANT
> *(as* VINCENTIO*)* Away, away, mad ass! His name is Lucentio
> and he is mine only son, and heir to the lands of me, Signior
> Vincentio.

VINCENTIO
> Lucentio! Oh, he hath murdered his master! Lay hold on
75 > him, I charge you in the Duke's name. O my son, my son!
> Tell me, thou villain, where is my son Lucentio?

TRANIO
> *(as* LUCENTIO*)* Call forth an officer.

Enter an Officer

> Carry this mad knave to the jail.—Father Baptista,
> I charge you see that he be forthcoming.

VINCENTIO
80 > Carry me to the jail?

GREMIO
> Stay, officer. He shall not go to prison.

BAPTISTA
> Talk not, Signior Gremio. I say he shall go to prison.

GREMIO
> Take heed, Signior Baptista, lest you be cony-catched in
> this business. I dare swear this is the right Vincentio.

MERCHANT
85 > *(as* VINCENTIO*)* Swear, if thou darest.

BAPTISTA

You're wrong, sir, very wrong. Why, what do you imagine his name to be?

VINCENTIO

His name! As if I wouldn't know his name, I who brought him up ever since he was three years old. His name is Tranio.

MERCHANT

(*as* VINCENTIO) Get rid of this mad fool! This is Lucentio, my only son and heir to all my lands.

VINCENTIO

Lucentio! Oh God, he's murdered his master! Restrain him! I charge you in the Duke's name. Oh, my son, my son! Tell me, you monster, where is my son Lucentio?

TRANIO

(*as* LUCENTIO) Call forth an officer.

An officer enters.

Take this mad wretch to jail.—Father-in-law Baptista, will you see that he's available to appear in court?

VINCENTIO

Take me off to jail?

GREMIO

Wait, officer. He mustn't go to prison.

BAPTISTA

Be quiet, Signior Gremio. I say he shall go to prison.

GREMIO

Be careful, Signior Baptista, lest you be made the dupe in this business. I could swear this is the real Vincentio.

MERCHANT

(*as* VINCENTIO) *Can* you swear to it?

GREMIO

Nay, I dare not swear it.

TRANIO

(*as* LUCENTIO) Then thou wert best say that I am not
Lucentio.

GREMIO

Yes, I know thee to be Signior Lucentio.

BAPTISTA

90   Away with the dotard! To the jail with him!

VINCENTIO

Thus strangers may be haled and abused.—O monstrous
villain!

Enter BIONDELLO, *with* LUCENTIO *and* BIANCA

BIONDELLO

O! We are spoiled and yonder he is! Deny him, forswear
him, or else we are all undone.

Exeunt BIONDELLO, TRANIO, *and* MERCHANT,
as fast as may be

LUCENTIO *and* BIANCA *kneel*

LUCENTIO

95   Pardon, sweet father.

VINCENTIO

Lives my sweet son?

BIANCA

Pardon, dear father.

BAPTISTA

How hast thou offended? Where is Lucentio?

LUCENTIO

Here's Lucentio, right son to the right Vincentio,

100   That have by marriage made thy daughter mine
While counterfeit supposes bleared thine eyne.

GREMIO

Well, no, not literally.

TRANIO

(as LUCENTIO) Then you'd better say that I'm not Lucentio.

GREMIO

No, I know that you're Signior Lucentio.

BAPTISTA

Away with the doddering fool! Take him off to jail!

VINCENTIO

Is this how strangers are treated here? You harass and abuse them?—This is unbelievable!

BIONDELLO *enters with* LUCENTIO *and* BIANCA.

BIONDELLO

We're ruined! There he is! Renounce him! Deny you know him or we're sunk.

BIONDELLO, TRANIO, *and* MERCHANT
exit as fast as possible.

LUCENTIO *and* BIANCA *kneel.*

LUCENTIO

Pardon, dear father.

VINCENTIO

Dear son, you're alive!

BIANCA

Pardon us, dear father.

BAPTISTA

Why? What have you done? Where is Lucentio?

LUCENTIO

Here is Lucentio, true son to the true Vincentio. I have made your daughter mine by marriage while false impressions blinded your eyes.

GREMIO
>Here's packing, with a witness, to deceive us all!

VINCENTIO
>Where is that damnèd villain, Tranio,
>That faced and braved me in this matter so?

BAPTISTA
105 >Why, tell me, is not this my Cambio?

BIANCA
>Cambio is changed into Lucentio.

LUCENTIO
>Love wrought these miracles. Bianca's love
>Made me exchange my state with Tranio,
>While he did bear my countenance in the town,
110 >And happily I have arrivèd at the last
>Unto the wishèd haven of my bliss.
>What Tranio did, myself enforced him to.
>Then pardon him, sweet father, for my sake.

VINCENTIO
>I'll slit the villain's nose that would have sent me to the jail.

BAPTISTA
115 >But do you hear, sir, have you married my daughter
>without asking my goodwill?

VINCENTIO
>Fear not, Baptista, we will content you. Go to. But I will in
>to be revenged for this villany.

Exit

BAPTISTA
>And I, to sound the depth of this knavery.

Exit

LUCENTIO
120 >Look not pale, Bianca. Thy father will not frown.

GREMIO

Quite the conspiracy! We've all been duped.

VINCENTIO

Where is that damned wretch, Tranio, who defied me in such a disgraceful manner?

BAPTISTA

Say, isn't this the Latin master Cambio?

BIANCA

Cambio is transformed into Lucentio.

LUCENTIO

It was love that performed these miracles. Bianca's love made me trade places with Tranio while he masqueraded as me around town. And now, finally, I've arrived happily at the blissful haven where I longed to be. What Tranio did, he did at my command. So pardon him, dear father, for my sake.

VINCENTIO

No, I'll slit the nose of the villain who would have sent me to jail.

BAPTISTA

But sir, have you married my daughter without my consent?

VINCENTIO

Don't worry, Baptista, you'll be perfectly satisfied. You'll see. Now I'm going inside to see that someone pays for this mischief.

He exits.

BAPTISTA

Me too—to see how far the mischief went.

He exits.

LUCENTIO

Don't worry, Bianca. Your father won't be angry.

Exeunt LUCENTIO *and* BIANCA

GREMIO
      My cake is dough, but I'll in among the rest,
      Out of hope of all but my share of the feast.

Exit

KATHERINE
      Husband, let's follow to see the end of this ado.

PETRUCHIO
      First kiss me, Kate, and we will.

KATHERINE
125   What, in the midst of the street?

PETRUCHIO
      What, art thou ashamed of me?

KATHERINE
      No, sir, God forbid, but ashamed to kiss.

PETRUCHIO
      Why, then let's home again. *(to* GRUMIO*)* Come, sirrah, let's
      away.

KATHERINE
130   Nay, I will give thee a kiss. *(kisses him)* Now pray thee, love,
      stay.

PETRUCHIO
      Is not this well? Come, my sweet Kate.
      Better once than never, for never too late.

Exeunt

LUCENTIO *and* BIANCA *exit.*

GREMIO

So much for my hopes! Well, I'll go in and join the others. All I can hope for now is a share of the feast.

He exits.

KATHERINE

Let's follow them to see how this turns out.

PETRUCHIO

First kiss me, Kate, and then we will.

KATHERINE

What, here in the middle of the street?

PETRUCHIO

Why not? Are you ashamed of me?

KATHERINE

Certainly not! But I'm ashamed to kiss, sir.

PETRUCHIO

All right then, back home we go. *(to* GRUMIO*)* Come, fellow, let's be off.

KATHERINE

No, wait. I *will* kiss you. *(kisses him)* Now please, love, stay.

PETRUCHIO

Isn't this good? Come, my sweet Kate. Better late than never—and it's never too late to change.

They exit.

ACT 5, SCENE 2

Enter BAPTISTA, VINCENTIO, GREMIO, *the* MERCHANT,
LUCENTIO, BIANCA, PETRUCHIO, KATHERINE, HORTENSIO,
WIDOW, TRANIO, BIONDELLO, *and* GRUMIO, *with the*
Servingmen bringing in a banquet

LUCENTIO
At last, though long, our jarring notes agree,
And time it is when raging war is done
To smile at 'scapes and perils overblown.
My fair Bianca, bid my father welcome,
5   While I with selfsame kindness welcome thine.
Brother Petruchio, sister Katherina,
And thou, Hortensio, with thy loving widow,
Feast with the best, and welcome to my house.
My banquet is to close our stomachs up,
10   After our great good cheer. Pray you, sit down,
For now we sit to chat as well as eat.

PETRUCHIO
Nothing but sit and sit, and eat and eat!

BAPTISTA
Padua affords this kindness, son Petruchio.

PETRUCHIO
Padua affords nothing but what is kind.

HORTENSIO
15   For both our sakes, I would that word were true.

PETRUCHIO
Now, for my life, Hortensio fears his widow.

ACT 5, SCENE 2

BAPTISTA, VINCENTIO, GREMIO, *the* MERCHANT,
LUCENTIO, BIANCA, PETRUCHIO, KATHERINE,
HORTENSIO, WIDOW, TRANIO, BIONDELLO, *and* GRUMIO
all enter, with the servants bringing in a banquet.

Everyone stands as LUCENTIO *proposes a toast.*

LUCENTIO

Finally, at long last, we've reconciled our differences.
Now is the time—when war is safely over—to laugh at
past dangers and adventures. My fair Bianca, bid my
father welcome, while I with equal affection welcome
yours. Brother Petruchio, sister Katherina, and you,
Hortensio, with your loving widow, you'll find no better entertainment anywhere. All of you are welcome
in my house. This last course here is for closing up the
stomach after great feasting. Now everyone be seated,
as this is the part where we sit and chat as well as eat.

PETRUCHIO

All we do is sit and sit and eat and eat.

BAPTISTA

Yes, Padua is famous for this pleasant life, Petruchio,
my son.

PETRUCHIO

Padua contains nothing that isn't pleasant.

HORTENSIO

I wish that were true for both our sakes!

PETRUCHIO

Well what do you know! Hortensio fears his widow.

*"Fears" here can
mean both "is
afraid of," which is
how Petruchio
means it, and
"frightens," which
is how the widow
takes it.*

WIDOW
Then never trust me if I be afeard.

PETRUCHIO
You are very sensible, and yet you miss my sense:
I mean, Hortensio is afeard of you.

WIDOW
20   He that is giddy thinks the world turns round.

PETRUCHIO
Roundly replied.

KATHERINE
Mistress, how mean you that?

WIDOW
Thus I conceive by him.

PETRUCHIO
Conceives by me? How likes Hortensio that?

HORTENSIO
25   My widow says, thus she conceives her tale.

PETRUCHIO
Very well mended. Kiss him for that, good widow.

KATHERINE
"He that is giddy thinks the world turns round"—
I pray you, tell me what you meant by that.

WIDOW
Your husband being troubled with a shrew
30   Measures my husband's sorrow by his woe.
And now you know my meaning.

KATHERINE
A very mean meaning.

WIDOW
                    Right, I mean you.

KATHERINE
And I am mean indeed, respecting you.

WIDOW

Me afraid of him? I don't think so.

PETRUCHIO

That's very sensible, but you missed my sense: I meant Hortensio is afraid of you.

WIDOW

He who is dizzy thinks the world is spinning.

PETRUCHIO

A very candid reply.

KATHERINE

What's that supposed to mean?

WIDOW

That's what I conceive of him.

"That's what I understand him to mean."

PETRUCHIO

Conceives by me? How does that sit with you, Hortensio?

"Conceives by me" = becomes pregnant by me.

HORTENSIO

My widow means that her remark expressed the way she understood him.

PETRUCHIO

Nice save! Kiss him for that, good widow.

KATHERINE

"He who is dizzy thinks the world is spinning"— please, tell me what you meant by that.

WIDOW

Your husband, being saddled with a shrew, projects his own suffering onto my husband. And now you know my meaning.

KATHERINE

A very nasty meaning.

WIDOW

My meaning *is* nasty, for it's you I mean.

KATHERINE

And I *am* nasty when it comes to you.

PETRUCHIO
> To her, Kate!

HORTENSIO
35   To her, widow!

PETRUCHIO
> A hundred marks, my Kate does put her down.

HORTENSIO
> That's my office.

PETRUCHIO
> Spoke like an officer! Ha' to thee, lad!

Drinks to HORTENSIO

BAPTISTA
> How likes Gremio these quick-witted folks?

GREMIO
40   Believe me, sir, they butt together well.

BIANCA
> Head and butt! An hasty-witted body
> Would say your head and butt were head and horn.

VINCENTIO
> Ay, mistress bride, hath that awakened you?

BIANCA
> Ay, but not frighted me. Therefore I'll sleep again.

PETRUCHIO
45   Nay, that you shall not. Since you have begun,
> Have at you for a bitter jest or two!

BIANCA
> Am I your bird? I mean to shift my bush,
> And then pursue me as you draw your bow.—
> You are welcome all.

Exeunt BIANCA, KATHERINE, *and* WIDOW

PETRUCHIO
You tell her, Kate!

HORTENSIO
You tell her, widow!

PETRUCHIO
I'll bet you a hundred marks, my Kate puts her flat on her back.

HORTENSIO
Well, that's really my job.

PETRUCHIO
Well said! Here's to you!

He drinks to HORTENSIO.

BAPTISTA
What do you think of these quick-witted folks, Gremio?

GREMIO
They certainly do like to butt heads!

BIANCA
A clever person would say their butting heads had horns on them.

Men whose wives cheat on them were supposed to have horns.

VINCENTIO
Ah, our bride has woken up!

BIANCA
Yes, but not out of fear. I'll go back to sleep now.

PETRUCHIO
No, you shall not. Since you chimed in, let's see if we can trade a caustic joke or two.

BIANCA
Am I the bird you're going to shoot at now? I'll move my bush, so you'll have to aim at a moving target. Thank you all for coming.

"Move my bush" = move to another bush (also with a sexual double entendre).

BIANCA, KATHERINE, *and* WIDOW *exit.*

PETRUCHIO

50   She hath prevented me. Here, Signior Tranio,
        This bird you aimed at, though you hit her not.—
        Therefore a health to all that shot and missed.

TRANIO

        Oh, sir, Lucentio slipped me like his greyhound,
        Which runs himself and catches for his master.

PETRUCHIO

55   A good swift simile, but something currish.

TRANIO

        'Tis well, sir, that you hunted for yourself.
        'Tis thought your deer does hold you at a bay.

BAPTISTA

        Oh, Oh, Petruchio! Tranio hits you now.

LUCENTIO

        I thank thee for that gird, good Tranio.

HORTENSIO

60   Confess, confess, hath he not hit you here?

PETRUCHIO

        He has a little galled me, I confess.
        And, as the jest did glance away from me,
        'Tis ten to one it maimed you two outright.

BAPTISTA

        Now, in good sadness, son Petruchio,
65   I think thou hast the veriest shrew of all.

PETRUCHIO

        Well, I say no. And therefore, for assurance,
        Let's each one send unto his wife;
        And he whose wife is most obedient
        To come at first when he doth send for her,
70   Shall win the wager which we will propose.

HORTENSIO

        Content. What's the wager?

PETRUCHIO

Well, she got away. Signior Tranio, you also took aim at that bird, though you didn't hit her.—So here's a health to all who've shot and missed.

TRANIO

Oh well, sir, I was really just like a greyhound that Lucentio let off the leash: I did the running, but the catch was his.

PETRUCHIO

A witty if a cynical reply.

TRANIO

It's good you hunted for yourself, sir. It's rumored that your deer holds you at bay.

When a deer turns and faces the pursuing hounds, it is said to be "at bay."

BAPTISTA

Oh-ho, Petruchio! Tranio got you that time.

LUCENTIO

I thank you for that quip, good Tranio.

HORTENSIO

Fess up, fess up, didn't that one strike home?

PETRUCHIO

He's made me a little sore, I'll admit. But since the gibe glanced off me, ten to one it hit you both straight on.

BAPTISTA

Seriously, though, son Petruchio, I think you have the most thoroughgoing shrew of us all.

PETRUCHIO

Well, I disagree. But why not put it to the test? Let's each one send for his wife. Whichever's is most obedient and comes most readily shall win the bet that we'll propose.

HORTENSIO

Agreed. What's the bet?

LUCENTIO
Twenty crowns.

PETRUCHIO
Twenty crowns?
I'll venture so much of my hawk or hound,
75 But twenty times so much upon my wife.

LUCENTIO
A hundred then.

HORTENSIO
Content.

PETRUCHIO
A match! 'Tis done.

HORTENSIO
Who shall begin?

LUCENTIO
80 That will I.
Go, Biondello, bid your mistress come to me.

BIONDELLO
I go.

Exit

BAPTISTA
Son, I'll be your half Bianca comes.

LUCENTIO
I'll have no halves. I'll bear it all myself.

Enter BIONDELLO

85 How now, what news?

BIONDELLO
Sir, my mistress sends you word
That she is busy, and she cannot come.

PETRUCHIO
How! "She's busy, and she cannot come!"
Is that an answer?

LUCENTIO

Twenty crowns.

PETRUCHIO

Twenty crowns? That's a bet I'd make on my hawk or my hound. I'd wager twenty times as much on my wife.

LUCENTIO

A hundred then.

HORTENSIO

Agreed.

PETRUCHIO

Good! It's a bet.

HORTENSIO

Who should begin?

LUCENTIO

I will. Biondello, go and tell your mistress to come to me.

BIONDELLO

Here I go.

He exits.

BAPTISTA

Son, I'll stake you half that Bianca comes.

LUCENTIO

I'll have no halves. I'll shoulder the whole bet.

BIONDELLO *enters.*

Well, what happened?

BIONDELLO

Sir, my mistress sends you word that she is busy and cannot come.

PETRUCHIO

What! "She's busy and cannot come!" Is that an answer?

GREMIO

90   Ay, and a kind one too.
            Pray God, sir, your wife send you not a worse.

PETRUCHIO

            I hope better.

HORTENSIO

            Sirrah Biondello, go and entreat my wife
            To come to me forthwith.

                                        Exit BIONDELLO

PETRUCHIO

95   O, ho, entreat her!
            Nay, then she must needs come.

HORTENSIO

            I am afraid, sir,
            Do what you can, yours will not be entreated.

            Enter BIONDELLO

            Now, where's my wife?

BIONDELLO

100   She says you have some goodly jest in hand.
            She will not come. She bids you come to her.

PETRUCHIO

            Worse and worse. She will not come!
            O vile, intolerable, not to be endured!—
            Sirrah Grumio, go to your mistress,
105   Say I command her to come to me.

                                        Exit GRUMIO

HORTENSIO

            I know her answer.

PETRUCHIO

                            What?

HORTENSIO

                                    She will not.

GREMIO

> Yes, and a nice one at that. Pray God your wife doesn't send you a worse one.

PETRUCHIO

> I'm hoping for better.

HORTENSIO

> You there, Biondello, go and request that my wife come to me straight away.

BIONDELLO exits.

PETRUCHIO

> Oh-ho, he *requests*! Why, then she'll have to come.

HORTENSIO

> I rather think, sir, that yours will not grant a request in any case.

BIONDELLO enters.

> So, where's my wife?

BIONDELLO

> She says she thinks this is a prank. She will not come. She says that you should come to her.

PETRUCHIO

> Worse and worse! She *will not* come! It's vile, intolerable, not to be endured!—You there, Grumio, go to your mistress. Say that I command her to come to me.

GRUMIO exits.

HORTENSIO

> I can guess her answer.

PETRUCHIO

> What?

HORTENSIO

> She will not.

PETRUCHIO
> The fouler fortune mine, and there an end.

Enter KATHERINE

BAPTISTA
> Now, by my holidam, here comes Katherina!

KATHERINE
> What is your will, sir, that you send for me?

PETRUCHIO
110 > Where is your sister, and Hortensio's wife?

KATHERINE
> They sit conferring by the parlor fire.

PETRUCHIO
> Go fetch them hither. If they deny to come,
> Swinge me them soundly forth unto their husbands.
> Away, I say, and bring them hither straight.

Exit KATHERINE

LUCENTIO
115 > Here is a wonder, if you talk of a wonder.

HORTENSIO
> And so it is. I wonder what it bodes.

PETRUCHIO
> Marry, peace it bodes, and love, and quiet life,
> And awful rule, and right supremacy,
> And, to be short, what not that's sweet and happy?

BAPTISTA
120 > Now, fair befall thee, good Petruchio!
> The wager thou hast won, and I will add
> Unto their losses twenty thousand crowns,
> Another dowry to another daughter,
> For she is changed as she had never been.

PETRUCHIO

The worse for me, no doubt about it.

KATHERINE enters.

BAPTISTA

By all that's holy, here comes Katherina!

KATHERINE

You sent for me, sir? Is there something you'd like me to do for you?

PETRUCHIO

Where are your sister and Hortensio's wife?

KATHERINE

They sit chatting by the parlor fire.

PETRUCHIO

Go bring them here. If they refuse to come, get physical—use a whip if you have to, but get them out here to their husbands. Go on, I said. Bring them here straight away.

KATHERINE exits.

LUCENTIO

This is a miracle, if you talk of miracles.

HORTENSIO

It is. I wonder what it means.

PETRUCHIO

I'll tell you what it means. It means peace and love and a quiet life, supremacy based on reverence and profound respect, and—not to go on and on about it—everything that's sweet and happy.

BAPTISTA

May good fortune come to you, good Petruchio! You've won the wager, and I will add twenty thousand crowns to what they owe you. Another dowry for another wife, for, truly, she is so transformed she's like a completely new woman.

PETRUCHIO

125   Nay, I will win my wager better yet,
       And show more sign of her obedience,
       Her new-built virtue and obedience.

       Enter KATHERINE, *with* BIANCA *and* WIDOW

       See where she comes and brings your froward wives
       As prisoners to her womanly persuasion.—
130   Katherine, that cap of yours becomes you not.
       Off with that bauble, throw it underfoot.

WIDOW

       Lord, let me never have a cause to sigh,
       Till I be brought to such a silly pass!

BIANCA

       Fie! What a foolish duty call you this?

LUCENTIO

135   I would your duty were as foolish too.
       The wisdom of your duty, fair Bianca,
       Hath cost me an hundred crowns since suppertime.

BIANCA

       The more fool you for laying on my duty.

PETRUCHIO

       Katherine, I charge thee, tell these headstrong women
140   What duty they do owe their lords and husbands.

WIDOW

       Come, come, you're mocking. We will have no telling.

PETRUCHIO

       Come on, I say, and first begin with her.

WIDOW

       She shall not.

PETRUCHIO

       I say she shall.—And first begin with her.

PETRUCHIO

Wait, I will win the wager more spectacularly, going even further to demonstrate her obedience, her newly created virtue and obedience.

KATHERINE *enters with* BIANCA *and* WIDOW.

Look, here she comes, with your ungovernable wives in tow, like prisoners of her womanly persuasion.— Katherine, that cap of yours doesn't look good on you. Take it off and throw it on the ground.

WIDOW

Lord, may I never see a day of trouble until the day I let someone treat me like that.

BIANCA

For shame! What kind of loyalty is this?

LUCENTIO

I wish your loyalty were as foolish. The wisdom of your loyalty, fair Bianca, has cost me a hundred crowns since dinner.

BIANCA

The more fool you for betting on my loyalty.

PETRUCHIO

Katherine, I'd like you to lecture these headstrong women on the nature of the loyalty they owe their lords and husbands.

WIDOW

You must be joking. There will be no lecture.

PETRUCHIO

Do it, I say. You can begin with her.

WIDOW

She shall not.

PETRUCHIO

I say she shall.—And first begin with her.

KATHERINE

145   Fie, fie! Unknit that threat'ning unkind brow
    And dart not scornful glances from those eyes
    To wound thy lord, thy king, thy governor.
    It blots thy beauty as frosts do bite the meads,
    Confounds thy fame as whirlwinds shake fair buds,
150   And in no sense is meet or amiable.
    A woman moved is like a fountain troubled,
    Muddy, ill-seeming, thick, bereft of beauty,
    And while it is so, none so dry or thirsty
    Will deign to sip or touch one drop of it.
155   Thy husband is thy lord, thy life, thy keeper,
    Thy head, thy sovereign, one that cares for thee,
    And for thy maintenance commits his body
    To painful labor both by sea and land,
    To watch the night in storms, the day in cold,
160   Whilst thou liest warm at home, secure and safe,
    And craves no other tribute at thy hands
    But love, fair looks and true obedience—
    Too little payment for so great a debt.
    Such duty as the subject owes the prince,
165   Even such a woman oweth to her husband.
    And when she is froward, peevish, sullen, sour,
    And not obedient to his honest will,
    What is she but a foul contending rebel
    And graceless traitor to her loving lord?
170   I am ashamed that women are so simple
    To offer war where they should kneel for peace;
    Or seek for rule, supremacy and sway
    When they are bound to serve, love, and obey.
    Why are our bodies soft and weak and smooth,
175   Unapt to toil and trouble in the world,
    But that our soft conditions and our hearts
    Should well agree with our external parts?
    Come, come, you froward and unable worms!

KATHERINE

Girls, girls! Wipe those frowns off your faces and stop rolling your eyes. This disrespectful stance toward the man who is your lord, your king, your governor tarnishes your beauty the way the frosts of winter blights the land. It mars your reputations as whirlwinds shake fair buds. And in no sense is it fitting or attractive. An angry woman is like an agitated fountain—muddy, unpleasant, lacking in beauty. And in this condition, no one—however dry or thirsty he may be—will stoop to sip or touch one drop of it. Your husband is your lord, your life, your keeper, your head, your sovereign, one who cares for you and who, for your ease and comfort, commits his body to harsh labor both on land and sea. Long, stormy nights at seas he stays awake, by day he endures cold while you lie safe and warm, secure in your beds at home. And in exchange he seeks no more from you but love, kind looks, and true obedience—too little payment for so great a debt. A woman owes her husband the same loyalty a subject owes his king. And when she is peevish and perverse, sullen, sour, and disobedient to his honest wishes, what is she but a loathsome, warlike rebel and an ungrateful traitor to her loving lord? I am ashamed that women are so foolish as to declare war when they should plead on their knees for peace, that they seek authority, supremacy, and power when they are under an obligation to serve, love, and obey. Why are our bodies soft and weak and smooth, unfit for toil and trouble in the world, if not so that our soft qualities and our hearts should agree with our external parts? Come, come, you weak, ungovernable worms!

My mind hath been as big as one of yours,
180 My heart as great, my reason haply more,
To bandy word for word and frown for frown.
But now I see our lances are but straws,
Our strength as weak, our weakness past compare,
That seeming to be most which we indeed least are.
185 Then vail your stomachs, for it is no boot,
And place your hands below your husband's foot:
In token of which duty, if he please,
My hand is ready, may it do him ease.

PETRUCHIO
Why, there's a wench! Come on and kiss me, Kate.

LUCENTIO
190 Well, go thy ways, old lad, for thou shalt ha 't.

VINCENTIO
'Tis a good hearing when children are toward.

LUCENTIO
But a harsh hearing when women are froward.

PETRUCHIO
(to LUCENTIO)
Come, Kate, we'll to bed.
We three are married, but you two are sped.
195 'Twas I won the wager, though you hit the white,
And, being a winner, God give you good night!

                    Exeunt PETRUCHIO *and* KATHERINE

HORTENSIO
Now, go thy ways, thou hast tamed a curst shrew.

LUCENTIO
'Tis a wonder, by your leave, she will be tamed so.

                                        Exeunt

My spirit has been as proud as each of yours, my courage as great, and my reason perhaps even better suited to bandy words back and forth and exchange frown for frown. But now I see our weapons are like straws, our strength like a straw's weakness, and our weakness past comparison, so that we seem to be the thing we most are not. Humble your pride, then, since it's useless, and place your hand beneath your husband's foot. As a gesture of my loyalty, my hand is ready if he cares to use it. May it bring him comfort.

PETRUCHIO

There, that's my girl! Come on and kiss me, Kate.

LUCENTIO

Congratulations, old pal, you've won the bet.

VINCENTIO

It's nice to see children playing well together.

LUCENTIO

But not so nice when women misbehave.

PETRUCHIO

Come, Kate, let's go to bed. We three are married, but you two are defeated. *(to* LUCENTIO*)* I was the one who won the wager, though you hit the white. And as the winner here I say good night.

Petruchio means the white circle at the center of an archery target, with a pun on Bianca's name, which means white.

PETRUCHIO *and* KATHERINE *exit.*

HORTENSIO

Well, congratulations. You've tamed a terrible shrew.

LUCENTIO

It's amazing, if I may say so, that she let herself be tamed.

They all exit.

SPARKNOTES LITERATURE GUIDES

Notes

Notes